BE THOU MADE WHOLE

BE THOU MADE
WHOLE

BY

GLENN CLARK

MACALESTER PARK PUBLISHING COMPANY

SAINT PAUL   MINNESOTA

BE THOU MADE WHOLE

By Glenn Clark

Copyright 1953
BY
MACALESTER PARK PUBLISHING COMPANY

First Edition 1953

Published in the United States of America by
Macalester Park Publishing Company
1571 Grand Avenue, St. Paul 5, Minnesota

FOREWORD

This book has an interesting history. It grew out of intimate conversations and prayers with people who were in need of healing. These conversations were expanded into letters, next were mimeographed for mailing to people in need, and finally they were bundled together as a Correspondence Course, given only to those who especially sought it.

Having been tried and tested in these various forms, they are now revised, re-edited, and in part completely re-written, and presented to the public in this book form.

I have spent a score of years studying and applying the "seven baths of Jordan" and long ago came to the conclusion that if anyone applied all seven of them successfully he would find himself healed of any ailment that flesh is heir to. When one has thoroughly bathed his soul, his mind, his emotions, his blood vessels, his lungs, his digestive tract, and his skin, there is very little room left for any germs of disease to get in their work.

This book is divided into lessons rather than chapters. The first three prepare and condition the student for the baths. The next seven lessons consist of the seven baths, which in turn prepare him for the two final lessons especially written for this book which it is hoped will "complete the job."

This book may be read fairly rapidly and completed in two or three days, or it may be made the basis for a complete "Course in Spiritual Therapy," continued for ten or twelve weeks covering the whole field of spiritual healing. In the latter case the "faculty" will consist, in addition to myself, of Agnes Sanford, Roland Brown, Starr Daily, and Rebecca Beard with laboratory experimentation, collateral reading and memorizing of vital passages.

As stated above this "course" grew out of informal conversations and lectures with folks in need. No attempt has been made to alter that simple and informal way of handling each subject. It is hoped that the reader will enjoy this informal, heart to heart relationship of author and reader.

GLENN CLARK

1571 Grand Avenue

St. Paul, Minnesota

September, 1953

CONTENTS

THE MAN OF YESTERDAY MEETS
THE MAN OF TOMORROW

Dear friend:

This is going to be a very personally-conducted course in spiritual and physical healing. I am going to do the very best I can for you. But because it is so personal and intimate you will have to excuse the informal way I handle it.

I haven't time to come to see you once a week for the next twelve weeks but I want you to imagine that I am actually taking a train each week and really seeing you in person. I want you to imagine that I am sitting beside you, talking to you intimately as I am actually doing right now in this letter. In one part of the lesson each week you will find that it sounds more like a lecture than a conversation, and that is exactly what it is. Occasionally I shall get up from the chair beside you, put my hands behind my back, and walk up and down the room, and do my best to hammer some new and very important truths on healing into your subconscious so deeply that you will never forget them. There is an advantage in my not being there and doing that in person, however, for if I did you would forget half of these important truths three hours after I got through telling them to you—if for no other reason, just because they are so new.

Yes, there are advantages in my not being there for in that way I am forced to write these truths down and you are forced to read them over and over again, whenever there is something important that you have forgotten.

After you have completed the reading of this book, you may wish to read it all over again, this time accompanying each lesson with the reading of another book. If you wish to do that the book assigned for this first lesson is the fascinating novel of Frances Hodgson Burnett, The Secret Garden. This book will "condition" your consciousness for the healing I hope will follow. It will make you turn and become as a little child, which was the first requirement, you may remember, that Jesus laid down for all those who wished to grasp His profound teachings on healthful living in the Kingdom of Heaven here and now. Read it as a little child would read it, for the sheer joy of the story, and with eager anticipation before beginning every chapter.

Well, now, I think my informal conversation with you is about over. I think I will get up and put my hands behind my back and walk up and down the room a while, and lecture to you on how to get well. So let's go!

Sincerely,

Glenn Clark

THE MAN OF YESTERDAY MEETS THE MAN OF TOMORROW

Man's organism was originally geared to the adventurous life of his cave man days. Unfortunately, it has remained so geared ever since. When primitive man was confronted by a pack of wolves, fear created within his body the necessary adjustments that enabled him to outrun or outsmart his foe. Mysterious secretions were released within his body which sent electric energy along his legs and speeded up the rhythm of his heart so that a power beyond his normal capacity was his. When a savage man attacked him, white anger seized him, which sent a stream of adrenalin into his blood, which in turn gave mighty strength to his fighting arm.

Using this power temporarily at his disposal, he made good his escape through fight or flight, and then with all his adrenalin safely drained from his system, he retired to his cave and slept as soundly as a babe.

Today when the fear of the wolves of unemployment seizes a man, the same adjustments take place within his body that enabled the cave man to outrun the wolves. But sitting dejectedly in his home, these superfluous adjustments glut his system with substances which he does not need. Not using them, they are converted into poisons, and the longer his anxiety continues, the more powerful the poisons become.

Resentment against a rival fills his blood with elements that would produce miracles if put to action, but in this prim and precise age it sets his inner membranes on fire with no compensating substance to quench the flame, and the longer the anger burns within him the hotter the flames become.

Primitive man gathered fish or eggs for immediate use. If he stored them in his cave for any length of time they would rot, and make his cave uninhabitable. There is something more terrible than living in the atmosphere of rotting eggs and decaying fish, however, and that is to live in the suffocating atmosphere of hate and fear.

Today our super-civilization is served by super-inventors with the result that an elaborate system of refrigeration has been devised to preserve unused eggs and fish for an indefinite length of time, but unfortunately, our super-inventors have not yet devised a similar system of refrigeration to take care of unused substances that our nervous system gathers together and releases in our blood stream when overtaken by anger or confronted with fear. Finding no elaborate refrigeration system in which to store these substances for safekeeping, the blood stream dumps them into the liver, the kidneys, the heart, and the lungs, with the passing remark, "Get rid of these rotting things if you can: I can't."

And there you are. What are you going to do about it?

There are two things you can do about it. One is: never get scared, never get angry, never harbor resentment or remorse or shame or jealous pride; in short, make yourself impervious to all the destructive emotions that man is heir to. That is another way of saying, make yourself into a saint or an angel. When men learn how to do that properly they may live forever. At any rate, scientists tell us that the body parts—from the bones to the tiniest cells—are so constructed that they should serve us well for five-hundred years if we keep the poisons out.

Another way of escaping or at least reducing the effect of those poisons is to work them off in uninhibited action—in other words, return directly or indirectly to the state of the cave man.

All this reveals to us that the only perfectly healthy creatures today are animals and angels. Mankind, shunted out into no-man's land, neither wholly of earth nor wholly of heaven, unable to give complete, unrepressed expression to his earthly impulsions, and not yet high enough in stature to live by heavenly impulsions alone, finds himself thwarted and frustrated on every hand.

Is there not some substitute method we can resort to, if we cannot use either the animal or angel method of getting rid of these poisons mentioned above? Wouldn't it do some good if, when confronted with fear of bank failure, the banker would go out after dark and run around the block, thus exorcising in a wholesome, natural way the substances his system secreted there by fear? The only drawback to this is that when one runs from a pack of wolves and escapes, the immediate danger is over and the fear subsides. But running around the block does not remove from the consciousness the fear of bank failures, so the fear poisons will continue to be secreted in the banker's body. Unless he can permanently drain off the fear, this method will keep him "running in circles," as the saying goes.

Suppose one were imaginative enough to associate a tree in his yard with someone who was his competitor in business, and whenever he found himself in a towering rage against his rival he gave vent to his pent-up energy by hacking at the tree, could that act head off a stroke of apoplexy or prevent the formation of a cancer? If after getting rid of his surplus adrenalin in this way he should forgive and feel sorry for the enemy he had so ruthlessly "cut down," then the cure *would* be complete. But if this physical exercise did not *exorcise* the demon of wrath from his system the relief would be merely temporary.

Thus we see, when all sources of relief and cure from these plagues which modern civilization has put upon him have been examined, that the only real and permanent healer is God, and the only sure escape from the poisons that flesh is heir to is to turn to the disciplines of a still higher civilization of the Soul.

As we begin our adventure let me surprise you with a new thought which should entice you: it is actually possible to step imaginatively, albeit temporarily, into the mould of the cave man on the one hand, and into the mould of the angel on the other, at regular intervals and in such a way that you will be kept in the pink of health and in the best of spirits. You cannot step into both moulds at the same time of course; the attempt would be like trying to straddle two horses at once. But it is a simple process. A man who goes fishing or hunting or mountain climbing all day Saturday gets a lot of poison centers cleared out in his mind and soul. Then if he follows this Saturday holiday with a Sabbath holy day of worship in church, prayer with friends, and the reading of books filled to the brim with "angel-atmosphere" the rhythm is complete.

William Wordsworth, nature-lover and poet, gives us the most perfect technique that can be found in literature for combining the cave man and the angel. No wonder he lived to a ripe old age. If you can catch the spirit which Wordsworth poured into the following lines, the reading of them will bring healing faster than any medicine. First let us see his portrayal of the cave man's response to nature in its purest and most innocent form:

> When first I came among these hills; like a roe
> I bounded o'er the mountains, by the sides
> Of the deep rivers, and the lonely streams,
> Wherever nature led; more like a man
> Flying from something that he dreads, than one
> Who sought the thing he loved. For nature then
> To me was all in all. I cannot paint
> What then I was. The sounding cataract
> Haunted me like a passion; the tall rock,
> The mountain, and the deep and gloomy wood,
> Their colors and their forms, were then to me
> An appetite; a feeling and a love,
> That had no need of a remoter charm,
> By thought supplied, nor any interest
> Unborrowed from the eye.

Now note his immediate transition to the *angelic* response to nature:

> That time is past,
> And all its aching joys are now no more,

And all its dizzy raptures. Not for this
Faint I, nor mourn nor murmur; other gifts
Have followed; for such loss, I would believe,
Abundant recompense. For I have learned
To look on nature, not as in the hour
Of thoughtless youth; but hearing oftentimes
The still, sad music of humanity,
Nor harsh nor grating, though of ample power
To chasten and subdue. And I have felt
A presence that disturbs me with the joy
Of elevated thoughts; a sense sublime
Of something far more deeply interfused,
Whose dwelling is the light of setting suns,
And the round ocean and the living air,
And the blue sky, and in the mind of man;
A motion and a spirit that impels
All thinking things, all objects of all thought,
And rolls through all things. Therefore am I still
A lover of the meadows and the woods,
And mountains; and of all that we behold
From this green earth; of all the mighty world
Of eye, and ear—both what they half create,
And what perceive; well pleased to recognize
In nature and the language of the sense,
The anchor of my purest thoughts, the nurse,
The guide, the guardian of my heart, and soul
Of all my moral being.

Notice how this union of one's soul with the soul
of nature can become a continuing, healing, inspiring process throughout the whole of life:

These beauteous forms,
Through a long absence, have not been to me
As is a landscape to a blind man's eyes;

But oft, in lonely rooms, and 'mid the din
Of towns and cities, I have owed to them
In hours of weariness, sensations sweet,
Felt in the blood, and felt along the heart;
And passing even into my purer mind,
With tranquil restoration—feelings too
Of remembered pleasure; such, perhaps,
As have no slight or trivial influence
On that best portion of a good man's life,
His little, nameless, unremembered acts
Of kindness and of love. Nor less, I trust,
To them I may have owed another gift,
Of aspect more sublime; that blessed mood,
In which the burthen of the mystery,
In which the heavy and the weary weight
Of all this unintelligible world,
Is lightened:—*That serene and blessed mood*
In which the affections gently lead us on—
Until, the breath of this corporeal frame
And even the motion of our human blood
Almost suspended, we are laid asleep
In body, and become a living soul:
While with an eye made quiet by the power
Of harmony, and the deep power of joy,
We see into the life of things.

In those emphasized words are great healing powers. They contain the three vital steps in healing:

First, turn your gaze upon God through beholding
His perfectly harmonious world of nature.
Second, completely forget your body and its seem-
ing limitations.
Third, hold this serenity without interruption for
a period of time.
But how can you hold it?

Through reading and re-reading lessons like this. By reading the books I shall prescribe for you each week. By going forth, and contemplating nature as Wordsworth did. Finally, by holding fast to a few basic truths and making them positive convictions and absolute knowing in your deepest subconscious mind. Here is such a truth. Read it and reread it until you *know* that it is true:

Scientists have discovered that the body is entirely renewed every eleven months. All the worn-out, run-down, or inefficiently working cells in your body can be completely replaced by brand new cells, filled with vitality and power, within a year's time, if you can control the reproduction of them at the source.

And what is the source?

Right thinking.

That is Scriptural. "As a man thinketh in his heart so is he." By "in his heart" is meant, "in his subconscious thinking." In other words, "in his knowing." But how can you *know* a thing? Not merely believe it but actually know it! One way is by looking at a thing so long, or repeating it so frequently, that you believe it. Wordsworth looked at God's handiwork in nature so often and so long that he melted and merged himself into it, until he became as whole as the Nature he looked upon. No wonder he lived to a "green old age."

The Bible is filled with promises that can help one to think "in his heart." Here is one to read and reread this week:

"Bless the Lord, O my soul;
And all that is within me, bless His holy name.
Bless the Lord, O my soul,

And forget not all His benefits:
Who forgiveth all thine iniquities;
Who healeth all thy diseases;
Who redeemeth thy life from destruction;
Who crowneth thee with lovingkindness and tender
    mercies;
Who satisfieth thy desire with good things,
So that thy youth is renewed like the eagle's."

EXERCISES FOR LESSON I *

READING EXERCISE: *The Secret Garden*. Gardening presents a splendid opportunity for the cave man-nature and the angel-nature to unite. Therefore, I recommend for outside reading this first week this book by Frances Hodgson Burnett. Read it for relaxation, for joy, and if you can't finish it in a week let it lap over with the next lesson.

MEMORIZING EXERCISE: Memorize the Twenty-third Psalm and verses one through seven of Psalm Ninety-one.

The selections for memorizing this week are the most healing Psalms in the entire Bible, and one rea-

* These exercises are designed for

    (1) Those who would like to expand this into a three months' study course to prepare them to bring healing to others.

    (2) Or those who are suffering from ill health themselves and would prefer the comfort of an armchair beside a shelf of books filled with interesting ideas to a hospital bed beside a shelf of bottles filled with uninteresting drugs.

Those taking the Short Course may omit the outside reading and be governed by their own choice regarding the memorizing, but they are especially urged to do the visualizing.

son is that they unite the release of the animal and the release of the angel in words of surpassing beauty. For instance, the Twenty-third Psalm is undergirded by the implicit trust of the sheep, the most helpless of all animals, and overgirded by the loving care of the Good Shepherd. The Ninety-first Psalm is undergirded by the release of the infinite trust of the eagle, the most powerful of all birds, and overgirded by the loving care of the heavenly angel who will "bear thee up."

VISUALIZATION EXERCISE: Every day for this week take a little period to imagine yourself playing some active game you have played in your youth or childhood. If you ever ran races, see yourself outspeeding all the other racers, but always easily and freely and in perfect *rhythm*. Or if your game was tennis, see yourself darting hither and thither on the court returning what to others would be impossible shots and always with easy rhythm. Or see yourself playing run-sheep-run or prisoners' base or jumping rope—but always rhythmically, easily, with a speed and endurance that amazes every onlooker. Just for fun imagine a great crowd looking on.

LESSON II

THE DIVINE LAW
OF WHOLENESS

Dear friend:

The theme of this lesson is Wholeness. Make it your resolve for an entire week to hold the thought of wholeness with you constantly. God comprises within Himself the whole world—yes, the whole universe. He made everything whole.

In contrast to God, man makes things in parts. Just watch a carpenter build a house. He nails a board to another board. Not so God. When He makes an oak tree the whole tree lies enclosed within the folds of the acorn, right from the very start. The whole child reposes in the little germ plasma in the mother's womb.

You were whole from the moment you were conceived. Everything about you from the very beginning was whole. It was and is God's will—His only will—for you to stay whole, and if you slip out of that wholeness for one moment all the forces of the universe are working together to pull you together again. "Acknowledge Him in all thy ways and He shall direct thy paths."

Let me repeat that—"all thy ways." Not your spiritual way only, but your physical way as well. Not just your way to church but your way home from church—even your way down the Jericho Road. When you fall among thieves who would rob you and strip you and open crevices in your tender skin, hold fast to the wholeness which God has bequeathed you.

For those who are taking this as a three months' study course, let me remind you that for you this is not a book but a series of lessons, with lectures, outside reading, and memorizing and visualizing exercises. The more time you can give to it the more value you will derive from it. Following every lesson, you are to spend a week doing the required reading before you undertake the next lesson. Read the entire series of lectures at once if you wish, but let every word sink in when you come back to them for re-reading.

Once a day this week, pray this prayer:

"Forgive me, Lord, for the little
crevices I have allowed to break into the
perfect wholeness You endowed me with.
Please forgive me and fill all those
crevices with Your healing Love so completely that henceforth I shall be impervious as in a citadel against disease or
discord of any kind. Amen."

Now give careful attention while you
listen to the following lecture. It will
hold a surprise for you.

Sincerely,

Glenn Clark

THE DIVINE LAW
OF WHOLENESS

The Divine Law is that everything should be whole, perfect, and complete. Anything that is whole is beautiful. Anything that is whole is true. A whole maple leaf is very beautiful, but tear it to bits and you destroy the beauty. Whole wheat is good. Remove some of the wholeness from the wheat, and its good nourishing power is largely lost. That which we leave to the laws of nature gravitates toward wholeness. If cracks or crevices come in the wholeness, nature undertakes at once to fill those cracks and crevices with elements which at first glance seem bad, but which, when carefully analyzed, prove to be nature's instruments for attempting to restore the wholeness. If we keep turned always to God, these cracks won't come, but when we forsake God and the cracks come, God does not forsake us. He sends in His salvaging crew of workers to clear the cracks of the debris that naturally accumulates in them. This "salvaging crew" consists of vermin to destroy dirt in cracks in barn floors, maggots to absorb poison in wounds, fevers to destroy infections in illness, mania to dull suffering in "split personalities." If we accept these rescue workers of nature in a friendly spirit, acknowledging their service and offering assistance to them, it is remarkable how obediently they will depart when their work is done.

When there are cracks in the barn floor and the vermin come in to destroy the decaying matter that falls into those cracks, don't condemn the vermin—

cement up the cracks! When there is a lesion in the body and infection develops, thank the fever that arises to help you burn out the infection, don't condemn it. The fever will leave when you drain out the infection. When a crack appears in a man's mind—a split in his personality—and mania appears as nature's anesthetic to dull the mental anguish that would otherwise be present, don't condemn the mania! Treat it kindly, as Jesus treated the demons of old, but when its job is done and the split personality is cemented over with the love of God and faith in the Healing Christ, thank the demon kindly and quietly but firmly command it to depart. When the plumber has cleared the obstruction in the kitchen sink he has absolutely no business to linger around.

A practical illustration of what I mean occurred in the First World War when a man terribly wounded on the battlefield was picked up hours later, and under the dirty wrappings of his bandages a young interne in the base hospital discovered the wound was filled with maggots. It was a hopeless case of gangrene, but when the physician in charge discovered the maggots, he commanded that the wrappings be replaced by clean ones but care should be used not to remove the maggots. The little creatures consumed the poison, and the patient recovered. Johns Hopkins Hospital honored this same physician for his discovery by putting him on its staff to breed maggots for special use in all cases similar to this, and the results have been marvelous.

A true physician of souls will see everything in this world and every person in this world as whole, perfect, and complete. Where there are any appearances of cracks or breaks, he will see God's hand, through direct intervention or through the indirect process of nature, filling these crevices and cracks in ways which, if properly understood, will always bring healing.

The kind of filler that God uses can be either positive or negative, depending entirely upon the state of consciousness of the person concerned. When one's state of consciousness is good, God sends the positive elements to fill these cracks: faith, hope, and love. If one has sufficient of these, no other filler is needed. Where the patient's consciousness is negative and his faith, hope, and love are inadequate for the purpose the negative elements enter in to do the job. The negative elements will depart, however, as soon as one becomes so surrendered to God that he can see good in everything, even in the negative elements and accepts them with understanding, forgiveness, gratitude, and love. That was the way the physician accepted the maggots and cured a broken body. That was the way Jesus accepted the demons and cured a broken mind. "I must decrease," said John the Baptist, for he depended upon denunciation, "and Christ must increase," for He depended upon love.

Jesus' way of handling demons in his day, and curing insanity in whatever form it presented itself to him, is a perfect illustration of what I am saying. He did not converse with demons in the spirit of hate, but in the spirit of friendliness; he did not combat them with anger; he commanded them with authority. This is exactly the way parents deal with refractory children, and masters deal with sullen servants. One of the four commissions that Jesus gave his disciples is described in the statement, "... gave them *authority* over unclean spirits." Ma... places where Jesus went people failed to recognize who he was, but the demons never failed to recognize him as the Son of God.

Jesus' technique of handling demons is very interesting. First he would find out the demon's name, just as the psychiatrist's first step today is locating in the subconscious the hidden cause of the psychosis. Having found its name, He could speak with authority, and the subconscious, always obedient to the voice of true authority, would quickly respond to his command. For instance, in one case the demon confessed that his name was legion. The word *legion* implied that there was no unity or wholeness in the man. He was split into a thousand different "selves." All Jesus needed to do was to cast out this disintegrating force called Legion, and putty up the crevices in the man with the great integrating force called Love, and the man was made completely whole. Jesus took pity on the demons, however, when they begged him to let them serve the world in some other place where a crack had occurred that might draw disease or pestilence upon others. Seeing some swine that were undoubtedly diseased, creatures which Moses in the ancient "unrefrigerated" days warned his people against touching, Jesus granted their request. The swine undoubtedly must have been infected or Jesus would never have allowed the demons to enter them. Had he not done so they would probably have started a pestilence that might have taken many lives. Demons are so

constituted that they can never enter into anything
or anyone where there are no "cracks" to receive
them.

In the Greek race, demons were actually considered helpers. Each philosopher had his private demon or guardian angel which he consulted. These
demons differed from the angels in only one way—
they warned their charges *against* evil, and didn't
show them the way *to* the good. The angels on the
other hand, whose eyes were too pure to behold iniq-
uity, led their wards only to the good.

The domesticated demons of Jesus' and Socrates'
day served as the left hand of God while the angels
served as the right hand. The demon of Socrates
turned on the red light to prevent accidents and as
a shield to ward off Karma. The guardian angel of
St. Paul turned on the green light to show the right
path and make the way straight for the triumph of
good. Demons make their appearance only after a
break is made in the perfect wholeness. They come
in to fill the crevices and cracks. The quick preven-
tive of all troubles, the way to cast out all demons
even before they appear, is to close all the crevices
in your soul and establish complete union with God
and man, and the way to do that is through the way
of love. Repent of your sins, forgive your enemies,
cast out all jealousy, resentment, lust, and hate, and
establish complete union with your brother through
love, and complete union with God through adoration and faith, and all forms of illness will stay
away. Jesus summed up all the laws and the prophets in his two great commandments, and he gave the

perfect rule for health and harmony when he stated the Golden Rule.

Some remarks are in order before you come to the exercises. There is going to be tremendous power in this healing course because we are going to marshall to our aid the two greatest instruments God has ever given man to use—imagination and faith. My own success in prayer comes largely from the fact that for thirty years I was a teacher of literature and creative writing and I there discovered that there were greater advantages in drenching oneself in poetry than in theology.

Prayers are only answered when the conscious *is in perfect alignment with the subconscious.* This is the theme of the first chapter of *I Will Lift Up Mine Eyes* where I show how the hind's sure-footedness on mountain heights comes from her rear feet always tracking perfectly with her front feet.

A man of great spiritual power wrote once:

"Prayers are not successfully made unless there is rapport between the conscious and subconscious mind of the operator. This is done through imagination and faith. Imagination and faith are the only faculties of mind needed to create objective conditions. Imagination is the beginning of the growth of all forms, and faith is the substance out of which they are formed."

Imagination, correctly used, does not *pretend* that which is not, it *sees* that which already *actually is.* Wholeness is the normal, natural, real thing, not a pretended thing. When you see yourself whole you are using your imagination creatively to see the exact true condition of your being. When you use your creative imagination to become aware of God's healing presence within you, this is not pretending, for God's presence *is* everywhere, omnipresent, omniscient, omnipotent. And where God is, all is whole, perfect, and complete.

Our theologians have been very slow to see that along with Jesus' towering faith also went a towering imagination. This is proved by the fact that the Sermon on the Mount has two beautiful allegories, one in the center about the lilies and birds, and one at the end about the houses built on sand and rock. And after this sermon he confined his teachings entirely to parables which created the form and furnished the faith, the "substance out of which they were formed."

Use your imagination and personify your ailment as a tiny little imp or a huge old demon, depending upon how small or large it seems to be. Having personified it you can easily call it forth and talk to it. Use this speech, or one similar to it:

"Thanks a lot, Mr. Demon, old top, for doing your very best to clean out every drop of fear, self-pity, or resentment or whatever it was that has caused these crevices to come. My only suggestion right now is when you apply your next cleansing job on some of my friends that you don't be quite so rough. But you can go now, for the Healing Christ is coming immediately to putty up all these crevices with His healing love. You always recognized his voice in the past and I know you will recognize it now, for He speaks kindly to you but always with irresistible authority. Come, dear Jesus, cast out the demon now that his job is done, and fill me completely. Thanks Jesus. Amen."

If you have an ailment or obsession to cast out, read this over every day for a week. Get that constructive imagination of yours to working.

EXERCISES FOR LESSON II

READING EXERCISE: *The Soul's Sincere Desire* is a book that came through me as a whole book, like Jesus' raiment, all of one piece and woven from above. Therefore I assign that for your reading this week. Keep it by your bedside and read as much or as little as you wish whenever you can. Read one chapter a day if you wish, or more rapidly if you prefer. Start each day by turning to the last chapter and reading (aloud if possible) one or more of the psalm-prayers at the close of the book. These psalm-prayers have been found to be very effective in closing crevices in the subconscious mind, and filling one with the healing wholeness that one needs.

MEMORIZING EXERCISE: In the first lesson we saw how Wordsworth closed all the crevices in his soul by finding absolute union with Nature. This week see if you can capture that quality of wholeness which Wordsworth caught by the memorizing of the psalm-prayer on wholeness in *The Soul's Sincere Desire*. Also complete the memorizing of the Ninety-first Psalm.

MEDITATION EXERCISE: No matter how the waves on the surface of the ocean roll and break, deep down in the center of the ocean all is calm and still. No matter how much you appear to be ailing and sick, deep down in the inmost center of you the real you is sound and well. Just as in compressed air the air can be compressed tighter and tighter when pressure is put upon it, so the outside pressures of life sometimes compress this inner you, this true body of health and wholeness within you into such small compass that it cannot be discerned by human eye, sometimes even by the doctors themselves.

Glenn Harding lay dying in Turkey with gangrene following a ruptured appendix. When all hope from human means was gone, he suddenly recognized this little body of inner life and realized that the more that liquid air is compressed the more irresistible will be its rebound the moment all pressure is removed. Thereupon he proceeded to remove all pressures—of fear, of doubt, of concern even for life itself, and put himself completely into the Father's hands. All pressure being removed, the rebound began—steady, irresistible, unstoppable, until the spark of life remaining within had expanded to fill his entire being, and perfect health returned. Out of his very weakness came perfect strength.

The reading of these psalm-prayers will have this effect. Each day you will sense this gradual rebound and spread of the consciousness of health deep within you. As that sense of wholeness spreads and expands gradually all the areas where the trouble seems to have been will feel its effects. The evil force will be expelled and the healing love of Christ will fill all the cracks and crevices until nothing but wholeness and health remains.

Then think on Love. Forgive anyone who ever did an unkind thing to you. Fill your entire being with the sweetness of Love. Love is the power that draws all things into perfectly adjusted and harmonious relationship with everything else. Just think! Every cell, every nerve, every organ brought into perfectly adjusted and harmonious relationship with every other cell, nerve, and organ in your entire body! So send out love to everybody. Then invite the peace of mind that passeth all understanding to come to you, and relax you in healing rest.

Lesson III

THE HEALING POWER
OF LIGHT AND WATER

Dear friend:

There are fourteen statements in the Bible describing peace as something that comes from or through God. Prayer is a force that takes its rise in man, a form of basic energy moving from the soul of man to the Soul of God. Love is a form of basic energy moving back and forth from man to God, and from God to man. But Peace is primarily a basic power that takes its rise in God and is bestowed by Him upon His creature man.

When one has exercised himself in prayer to God, when he has immersed himself in love for God, the next step is to come into stillness in the presence of God and await the coming of the Peace that passeth all understanding, straight from the heart of God.

The smallest measure of that peace brings contentment in the waiting; a larger measure is assurance of full pardon and full healing; a still larger measure is the blessed sense of union with God and all mankind; and the largest measure of all brings Pentecost.

This peace may not allay all pain at once, it may not bring an end to all hardship and need for continuing endeavor. "Peace I give unto you," said Jesus. "My peace I give unto you, not as the world giveth, give I unto you."

This heavenly peace, the gift of God, is not to be confused with earthly peace, which at best is but a spurious counterfeit and make-believe of the real thing. Indeed the only bona fide real peace is the peace that comes from above.

Because it is the one special monopoly of God Himself it is the most precious gift that God can bestow. When you find yourself recipient of it your heart should overflow in gratitude. For it is evidence that all your prayers are being answered. It is proof that only the love of God and the love of your friends can reach you. It is assurance

—at least as long as that peace encompasses you—that you are as impervious to any earthly harm as though you were in a citadel. And in its most overpowering visitation it is assurance that you are a branch of the living vine, a drop in the eternal ocean—that you and the Father are One.

What are some of the things that destroy Peace? Anger and Fear are the most aggressive enemies of Peace. But when anger is turned into forgivingness and fear into trustingness, God sends His most powerful Peace to reward the forgiver and the truster.

Guilt and Remorse are both great peace destroyers. But when Guilt is changed to sincere repentance, and wistful longing for forgiveness takes the place of remorse, tremendous Power comes into play. For that wistfulness carries within itself the seeds of atonement and compensation. When Guilt and Remorse cease their agony and reach forth with wistfulness to restore the ones who are wronged, then great is the power thereof.

When Peace is powerful enough to overcome Anger or Fear or Guilt or Remorse, you can rest assured that it is a Peace actually sent from God—the Peace that passeth all understanding—the Peace that sweeps away all evil and builds a new heaven and a new earth, no matter where you are.

Faithfully,

Glenn Clark

THE HEALING POWER
OF LIGHT AND WATER

Cracks and crevices in the body as well as in the soul are best cleansed by generous application of water and sunshine. Vermin find nothing to feed on where all is scrubbed clean. Germs and maggots vanish when the sunshine is let in with all its power. So the first step in healing lies in proper bathing of all the cracks and crevices. Elisha undoubtedly knew what he was talking about when he commanded Naaman to bathe *seven* times in the River Jordan. For did you realize that after each bath the very act of stepping out of the water preliminary to entering it again was plunging him into a sunbath as completely as the moment before he had plunged into a water bath? After each exposure of his naked body to the cleansing of the water he was thus automatically exposing his naked body to the healing power of the sunlight. Can it be that this is the reason Elisha commanded *seven consecutive* baths instead of *one prolonged bath?*

Let us look at this fact steadily until we discern the great truth concealed within it. Can it be that in this sevenfold alternating rhythm of sunshine and water lies the perfect secret of the healing art?

In the first lesson I said, "All this reveals to us that the only perfectly healthy creatures today are animals and angels." When we look for their secret shall we not find that animals keep well through sunshine and water, and angels keep holy through the equivalents of sunshine and water: love and humility?

Consider for a moment the marvelous life-giving power contained in these two elements, light and water. First let us look at the power of light.

Light is the source of all life.

The earth was created from the sun. It was originally thrown out from its womb, and ever after has turned toward its mother like a child at the breast, to derive its substance entirely from its parent source. And ever since the earth was made, everything upon the earth that has life turns to the sun as the source of that life.

The lily of the field looks up toward the sun, and from its light, through some primary inner alchemy which nature has endowed the lily with, converts the life of the sun into life of its own, for its own sustenance. The cow and sheep, not being blessed with this primary alchemy which enables the lily to take its sustenance at first hand from the sun, have to turn to the lily itself, and to other growing plants of the field, and by eating them, absorbs, at second hand, the light of the sun. From this grass we say they draw their life, but in reality it is from the sun that all their life comes. The sun filters through the porous blades of the grass, and thus enters into the flesh and blood of the flocks that roam the fields.

Man, still further removed from the elementary alchemy of nature, is not satisfied with eating grass alone, and other products of the field, but turns to the cattle and the sheep which have taken the light of the sun at second hand and by devouring them in the form of beef and mutton he derives sustenance from the sun at third hand.

Thus all things insofar as they wish to live find themselves turning toward the sun as the ultimate source of all life.

Now prayer in its simplest form is merely turning toward God as the source of all one's life. In a later lesson we shall explain this more fully.

The lily of the field, reaching up toward the light, is in a continuous act of prayer. The cattle of the field, with heads bowed above the herbage, are also in an act of prayer, for they too, are turning toward their source of life. And so, when we bow our heads above the food on our tables, before a single word of grace has been uttered, we are, if we only knew it, also turning, and let us hope with gratitude, toward the source of our life.

Men have sought high and low for dependable, sure cures for every ailment under the sun, only to find that the last and ultimate and final remedy that surpasses all remedies lies right in the sun itself. In other words, no matter in what specific, particular, concrete form the remedy is discovered, it is found to have its source in the ultra-violet rays of the sun.

Tuberculosis, which doctors used to try to smother under covers and curtains and closed doors and drugs, while the patients died like locusts, is now found to possess no power of resistance whatever against the simple, ultra-violet light of the sun. Radium, which has similar power and which has long been the chief hope of the cancer sufferers, is also a mere derivative of the sun. Wounds which we buried under smears of salve and vaseline are now seen to heal much faster when exposed to the sun and air.

The worst breeding grounds of contagion are found to be darkened tenements or abodes where the sun cannot penetrate.

X-ray treatments is another process of turning on the light. Increasing the window space increases efficiency in homes and factories. All these things tell the story of the ever increasing discoveries of the healing power of the sun.

One by one the strongholds of disease have given away before this one all-conquering remedy of simple sunlight, until it begins to appear that no disease need master a person provided he can just let enough sunlight in.

X-ray treatment is merely a method of treatment by "canned sunlight" so to speak. The same with radium, the same with cod liver oil. Cod liver oil, which for a long time was accepted as the "king of all medicines" for restoring vitality in children and invalids, derives all its virtue from the fact that it is nothing more or less than "bottled sunshine." In the words of Professor Henry Steenbock of the University of Wisconsin, "It derives its virtue from the fact that the ultra-violet rays of the sun penetrate the water and so irradiate the codfish." Iron is another property of the sun. Doctors are beginning to cease feeding iron to patients in its medicinal or inorganic form, and are feeding it to them rather in the form of cabbage, tomatoes, and oranges, the vegetables which reach up or hang up in the sunlight and drink in its rays. They are the products that are most conspicuously interpenetrated with the ultra-violet rays of the sun. These are more life-giving than the more starchy foods such as potatoes, which lie embedded deep in the ground.

To keep healthy, then, to build up health after one is sick, you should live in the sun, abide in the sun, and let it sink and abide in you. Have your living quarters irradiated by the sun's rays, eat vegetables, fruits, and all foods that grow in the sun and are irradiated with the sun, and when disease does come, get the sunlight in contact with it, or take vitamins or medicines which derive their value from the ultra-violet rays of the sun.

For sickness let us have light; for ignorance, light; for vice, light. Light then, is the source of all healing. When Jesus healed men by saying, "Thy sins are forgiven," was he doing anything else than taking them forth and turning on the light so strong that neither sin nor sickness could exist in its presence? For to him, the light of the physical world was merely the symbol of the light of the inner world.

Water and sunlight are the source of all life, and life at its source is never sick, never old, never diseased. The nearer we get to the source of all life, and the more we are able to identify ourselves with it, the younger and healthier we shall become.

Now let us turn our attention to the healing power of water.

Nothing on this earth can live outside of water. Fish are not the only creatures entirely dependent upon that element. Man as an embryo in the mother's womb is a water creature as much as any creature of the sea. When he emerges into the outer world he still carries the water with him. His skin and exterior texture is merely a container that holds the water of which he is still 95% composed.

The life of everything upon this earth is in the water it contains, although in the tree it goes under the name of sap, and in man under the name of blood. Remove the sap, remove the blood, you remove the life. But not only is the fluid part of man mostly water, even the so-called solidified parts of his body, his muscles and sinews, are about 95% water.

The egg has nothing solid in it, and yet by the transformation wrought by twenty-one days of brooding warmth of the setting hen, there comes forth a little chick with solid bones and feathers that certainly do not look like water nor feel like water. And yet from purely fluid elements all this solid came.

Even as I am writing this Lesson word comes out of Russia telling how a great physician there has discovered how people could live to be 120 years of age. "The secret lies," he says, "in keeping the connecting tissues between the organs of the body from drying out"—in short, keeping these tissues liquid, fluid, filled with sap.

Just as the best way to correct a defective coin is to send it back to the mint and have it melted down into its original pattern and recast in perfect form, so if anything is the matter with the body, the surest and quickest cure would be wrought by returning it to the fluid state in which it began, if it were possible to do this, even returning it to its prenatal fluid state, and there have the trouble adjusted at the source. Nicodemus understood Jesus to mean exactly that when he told him that he should be born again. But while Jesus never intended to imply that one should return again into his mother's womb, he did say that if one wished to enter the Kingdom of Heaven he should turn and become as a little child.

The simplest as well as the surest way to get cleansed of all sin, sickness, or other betraying evils is to melt oneself down as the old coin is melted down at the mint and comes forth fresh and new. And how can we melt ourselves down and come forth in original form better than by turning and becoming as near as possible like a little child? If an old gnarled tree that has stood for a hundred years bears brand-new leaves each spring which are as fresh and new as the original sprout that sprang from the ground, a tree thus holding within itself the capacity for rebirth and constant renewal, why don't we investigate ourselves and see whether we too may possess within ourselves somewhere a fountain of ever-renewing life?

If our bodies are too solid to change immediately let us see what we can do with our minds. Just see what happens when we make our thoughts like the thoughts of a little child. A child is full of day-dreams, and loves to look expectantly ahead with the sense of wonder. A person who continues to look at life with expectancy and wonder never grows old. An old person's thoughts get into ruts, he thinks in frames. Anything that is put into a frame can be broken. As long as it is fluid and flowing it cannot be hurt. Therefore, certain mannerisms or habits of thought should be cast overboard, especially if they are merely hashing and rehashing the same old ideas, same old prejudices and same old traditions. Open up to new thoughts and new hobbies through entering new fields of knowledge, reading new books, seeing new sights, travelling to new places. A child expects a new adventure each day. One way to keep forever well and forever young is to expect some new thing each day, or do some new thing, or read some new thing, or at least dream some new thing.

Just see what would happen if one kept his emotions young. Let us take the emotion of love and make it as pure, spontaneous, genuine, and released as the love of a little child. A little child has no hypocrisy in his loves. Grownups have to be on their guard and pretend to love people of prominence or of social position, when they don't really love them. Hypocrisy is one of the most aging of all things. It is a carrying of outer shells; and outer shells create age—in fact, all that age is is outer shells that we allow to creep over us.

A little child has no lust in his loves, that lust which drains vitality and wears one out. Little children do not love people to get something out of them, are not filled with intrigue and cupidity. Take hypocrisy, lust, greed, and vanity out of your love, and love is the most health-creating emotion there is. Then cast out fear, jealousy, hate, resentment, remorse, self-pity, and the habit of criticism, and you have removed most of the age-creating, sickness-breeding emotions there are.

All these methods of making the emotions and thoughts young are merely other ways of saying, making them more fluid and more flowing and more like water. In other words, put your old, sick emotions and old, sick thoughts to soak just as you would your drying lettuce, and let them come forth again crisp and fresh and flowing and brand-new. That is what is meant by being reborn. Here are some exercises that will help you. They will give you opportunity to exercise your imagination like a little child, using the symbols of the sun and water.

EXERCISES FOR LESSON III

READING EXERCISE: *The Thought Farthest Out.* This is a very "fluid book." As it contains seven chapters why not read a chapter a day?

MEMORIZING EXERCISE: Memorize one section of the Divine Plan each day.

VISUALIZATION EXERCISE: *Exercise 1*—First, close your eyes and imagine yourself wading out into a lake—not a lake of water this time, but a lake of God's Spirit. Picture your feet becoming immersed, then your ankles, then your body, taking each part of the body in turn until finally you are completely immersed in the Spirit, and are floating effortlessly in it. Let go your tensions of body, let them all be washed away in this soft, penetrating water. Then let the tensions of your mind and soul be washed away. All your sins and errors and fears and selfishness—completely washed away. Then command your problems, yes, all your troubles to be completely washed away. Relax your thoughts. Relax your emotions. Relax your soul. Let your Hope be melted into God's Hope, your Love into God's Love, yourself into God's Self.

Don't smile at this. This immersion in Jordan, even in thought, can be very transforming.

Exercise II—Now having experienced the healing power of water through wading out into it in imagination, immersing yourself in it, losing yourself in it, becoming one with it, try the same experience with sunshine. As the spiritual qualities which water represents are selflessness, spontaneity, purity, and childlikeness, the spiritual qualities that sunshine represents are love and joy.

Here is an exercise of the imagination that will not only develop you greatly spiritually, but will have a great effect in keeping you sound and well. For one week take this exercise daily.

Think of yourself as a drop of water in the mud-puddle that is filled with dirt, microbes, and germs of all kinds. When the drop of water wants to become clean and pure it does not have to consult the doctor or depend on surgery or medicine, provided —note this word *provided*—it gives itself to the drawing power of the Sun's rays. The instant it does this it is drawn up into cleanness and purification. That moment it becomes sound and well.

What is the spiritual counterpart of this distilling process of the drop of water? It is to give yourself without reservation to the drawing power of the Love and Joy of God. Think of yourself as just as wonderful as a drop of water. Then give yourself to the drawing power of God and in imagination feel yourself being drawn up out of all your troubles. To sharpen your consciousness of the drawing power of God's rays of Love for you and of your rays of love for God, read marked passages from the teachings of Jesus, the Psalms, or books that have helped you, and give yourself to their drawing power. These Psalms in the Bible make excellent "elevators"; the 23rd, the 121st, the 91st, the 103rd, the 51st. Everyone should know of other passages in the Bible that serve this purpose best for him.

Try reading aloud these psalms that lift you until they become a part of your consciousness. As a sense of peace comes to you this is the surest sign that you are actually being "drawn up."

Think of your body thus drawn up, as a completely relinquished drop of water being drawn up by the sun's rays, and converted into dew-water, as pure as crystal, as pure as the very clouds of heaven.

Then think upon this body filled with illumination as overflowing with Love and the golden Joy of God—radiating the light of His glorious Sun.

Think of yourself as this water-body, as fresh and new and young as the youngest child, transparent, incandescent, unable to hold sickness or sin or one impure thought. Think of yourself as this sun-body, beautiful, glorified, reflected and reflecting the light of God, His intelligence, love, beauty, health, and vigor.

It is the Divine Self within us that illumes the face, the rising or coming forth of the sun of righteousness with healing in its beam—the emerging of the Body Electric. Arise, shine! Your light has come! The Body Electric is here! It is yours! If you are able to see this clearly enough, to realize absolutely how your body is a mere emanation of pure water and pure sun, your glorious being will uncover its beauty and splendor with such brightness and effulgence that mortal eyes about you could not stand its beams—the glory of the transcendent expression of the Light of God. All centers of infection or symptoms of ill-health would vanish like dew before the sun.

When Jesus stepped into this realization on Mt. Herman his garments shone as a fuller's cloth and his disciples could not look upon him for the glory was so great. "And I, if I be lifted up," said Jesus, "will draw all men unto me." You are one of those "men," experiencing the drawing power of the Son of God. As the drop of water keeps its eyes upon the sun, keep your eyes upon the Son and let Him draw you into higher realms of glory.

Lesson IV

THE FIRST BATH:
BATHING THE SOUL

Dear friend:

There is nothing more thrilling than the awareness that one abides in God and God abides in him. Most of the events of life are so trivial. Most of the motions we make are waste motions. But every moment we spend with God brings permanent values. "This is the life eternal, to know God and Jesus Christ whom He hath sent." Nothing can be added to such moments and nothing can be taken from them.

Supposing that you have not improved in health in the past weeks but through these exercises have grown closer in touch with your Father. The time, you will soon find, has been well spent. Sometimes after months of laying foundations of the Spirit the outer healing suddenly takes place. I wore spectacles for forty years. After praying a few times for my eyes without seeming effect I ceased praying for myself and prayed for others. I didn't bother to pray for my eyes again. Instead I immersed myself in the Love of God. I was too busy trying to help others to find time to think of myself. I was in such ecstasy over finding ever-increasing union with Reality--with the Holy Spirit-- that I considered my bad astigmatism a trivial matter. Then one day a taxi driver slammed a door in my face and smashed my glasses. I was away from home for that week and wondered how I could get along without their aid. I didn't need to wonder. I didn't need to be provoked with the chauffeur. The Lord had arranged a surprise for me. I didn't need the glasses any more. I now put on a pair only when I read. Maybe that is just a superstition about sixty-year-olders that the race may outgrow.

Keep on building your spiritual foundation. Perhaps the Lord is preparing a surprise for you. It may happen before you complete the lesson this very week.

But hold fast to this--the important thing is to keep centered in God.

Now you are ready for the first Bath—
the Bath of the Soul.

So up I go and start that lecture
again. And this is an important one!

Sincerely yours,

Glenn Clark

THE FIRST BATH:
BATHING THE SOUL

Strange it is after the miracle of Naaman's healing that no mention is made in the Old Testament of anyone ever again bathing in the River Jordan. One would think that crowds would have literally flocked there after they heard how it cured Naaman. That is exactly what they did do but not until a thousand years later, long after the records of the Old Testament had closed. It was not until the records of the New Testament had begun and then not because of what Elisha said but because of what a new prophet was saying. When the crowds did start down to Jordan again they were drawn there not to be healed physically but to be healed spiritually. Not until John the Baptist came along do we read of anyone being immersed again in the waters of Jordan.

But John's command differs from Elisha's in that instead of the word *bathe* he uses the word *baptize*. As "bathe" is the "trademark" of the physical bath, *baptize* is the "trademark" of the spiritual bath. Another difference in the command of John is that instead of asking us to take *seven* baths he asks for only *one*. However, that one—and this is largely overlooked by modern theologians—included the two phases of water and sunlight that we have considered at such length in Lesson II or as John put it, "water and fire."

In the third chapter of Matthew the eleventh verse, we read the testimony of John the Baptist regarding these two essential ingredients of the perfect baptism:

"I indeed baptize you with *water* unto repentance; but He that cometh after me is mightier than I, whose shoes I am not worthy to bear. He shall baptize you with the *Holy Ghost, and with Fire.*" As the moon derives its light from the sun, so John derived his light from Jesus. As water is controlled by the moon and fire is controlled by the sun, the baptism of John washes away the evil and the baptism of Jesus pours in the good. To be baptized with water is to be cleansed of imperfection; to be baptized with the Holy Ghost and with Fire is to receive perfection.

Let us look first at the baptism with water. The spiritual symbolism of this is the casting out of all sin from the soul. Two words loom very large in this process: repentance and forgiveness. One of the most healing experiences that anyone can go through is the discovery that perfect repentance is always followed by perfect forgiveness. When we *repent* of all our sins, God *forgives* all our sins. And following perfect repentance with perfect forgiveness, comes perfect healing. It was not by mere accident that the psalmist placed the following phrases in immediate sequence: "Who forgiveth all thine iniquities; who healeth all thy diseases; who redeemeth thy life from destruction."

Not only must *God* forgive our sins, but *we* also must forgive our sins. One of the hardest things for a conscientious person to do is to forgive himself for mistakes that he has made. Had the paralytic been able to have done that he might have been healed by the mere hearing of the Sermon on the Mount; and just think how that would have saved his four friends all the inconvenience of letting him down through the tiled roof!

Not only must one be able to forgive oneself following his baptism of repentance, but he must be able to forgive others likewise. Stanley Jones in *Is the Kingdom of God Realism?* ranks the sense of guilt as one of the chief causes of illnesses, and Agnes Sanford has found in her rich experience of healing that the forgiving of others is the key that unlocks the door that lets in the healing power more than anything else.

The baptism with water is man's individual effort to cleanse himself from the imperfection of himself. But if he stops there he is incomplete. From then on he will feel increased responsibility for his acts and will try his best to keep from sinning again. For as long as he is the creator of his own results he shall continue to find himself in need of more repentance. Not until one is baptized with the Holy Ghost and with Fire will he find the fusion beginning to take place between him and the Father, and begin to experience the blessing of abiding in the Father as the Father abides in him. From then on he will be like the branch on the vine. Henceforth as the vine moves the branch moves. He will begin to live in the Eternal Light of God, in which there is no darkness, neither shadows that are cast by turning. He will wake up each morning as a little babe, free from care and full of trust, knowing that he is a Son of God; he will retire at night glorifying the splendor of the day, filled with gratitude and joy that he and the

Father are One. In this divine partnership he will
recognize that his particular job is to look after the
intentions and that God's particular job is to look
after the results. Thus nothing matters excepting
that he hold fast to that union with God. Whether
it comes by the burning coals placed upon his lips or
by the fire of faith placed in his heart, it will mean
that henceforth he is but a channel for the outwork-
ing of the plan of God. If one can achieve this state
of consciousness, if one has experienced this first
bath of the Jordan, in other words, the baptism of
the soul by the water of cleansing and the baptism
of the spirit by the fire of inspiration, he can be
healed of all disease.

In the fourteenth chapter of Leviticus, the process
of the Bath of the Spirit is perfectly outlined for us
in a beautiful spiritual allegory. The ceremonial
law of permanent spiritual cleansing following the
physical healing is as follows:

"Then shall the priest command to take for him
that is to be cleansed two birds alive and clean . . .
and the priest shall command that one of the birds
be killed . . . as for the living bird, he shall take
it . . . and shall dip it in the blood of the bird that
was killed; . . . and he shall sprinkle upon him
that is to be cleansed of the leprosy seven times, and
he shall pronounce him clean, and shall let the living bird loose into the open field . . . and he shall
be clean."

These two birds represent the spirit of these two
baths we have been considering. They represent the
two conceptions a sick person can take of himself.
One bird represents, for instance, the sick condition

in which he *appears* to the outside world; that picture must be destroyed, denied, and cast aside. The *other* bird represents the way he *actually is* in the sight of God, made after His image and likeness, a perfect being in a perfect world, governed by a perfect God.

But while the first bird is denied and cast from the consciousness, the values that can be extracted from the illness must not be denied. These values are to be carefully treasured and pondered upon for seven days. The sprinkling of the blood of the slain bird upon the sick person "seven times" is a symbolical way of saying that after one has completely destroyed the view of himself as a sick man, and thrown it away, he should hold fast to the values that such an experience has brought him.

This is the point where most spiritual healers fail. They try to cast aside the entire thought of the illness as nothing but evil, as something that should be forgotten and despised and gotten rid of as quickly as possible. They forget that if God does all things, He permits us to go through such experiences for a purpose, and we have not really met His will until we find that purpose and gratefully accept it.

Was your illness sent to sprinkle patience into your consciousness, or love, or tolerance, or humility, or obedience? Was the illness to turn you to God? If it accomplished that you surely should be glad that you were allowed seven days for sprinkling a lot of gratitude for that blessing. Did you learn how to pray? Were some friends drawn to you closer than ever? Did the Bible and spiritual books take on new meanings for you? Did the illness make you more humble, more loving, more wise? Did it open your eyes to deeper visions, to greater faith, to greater appreciation of the presence of God in your life?

When you have found the good that has come to you from your illness, there will automatically be removed from your soul all resentment, worry, impatience, and pride, and you will be ready to move ahead, a cleansed and perfected soul. Then you will have learned the lesson your illness was sent to bring you.

The first bird represents the baptism by water, the baptism that washes away the bad. But in this case the water has been transformed into blood, and a sprinkling by blood transcends a baptism by water in that it not only cleanses but it atones, it not only washes away the bad but it also preserves all the values which the experience with the bad has brought.

Having accepted the baptism by water and blood, now let us turn to the baptism by the Spirit and the Fire. There is a legend of a bird called the Phoenix Bird that constantly goes up in flames and then rises again from its own ashes—a symbol of constant resurrection and constant rebirth. The second bird referred to in Leviticus typifies the healing qualities of the Phoenix Bird, the sound, reborn body emerging out of the experience which illness has wrought. This allegory has a vital message for us at this point, which is as follows: As much as we sincerely, yes, eagerly desire the complete health which this bird typifies, we must not *press down* too hard in our de-

mands that it come to pass. We must vision it clearly
and hopefully each day for seven days while using it
to sprinkle over our consciousness a greater awareness and a deeper gratitude for the values the temporary illness has brought. Then after seven days of
holding this Soul's sincere desire to our heart, we
must be so surrendered to the will of God that we
shall be willing to relinquish it entirely into the
Father's hands.

After the seven days of prayer of gratitude are
over, take your vision of a perfect body and "let go"
even of that, yes, set it free in the "open field" of
God. In other words, be willing, even as Abraham
was willing to sacrifice his son if God so commanded,
to give up with radiant acquiescence your dream of
physical wholeness. Offer it to Him, saying,
"Father, now that I am sprinkled with the full values
that this sickness can bring me, I am so grateful
that I am willing to relinquish even my desire to get
well if You have in mind some larger plan or some
greater good than I can see. I shall turn over to You
now this vision of the well person that I have been
holding for a week, and for the rest of the time I
want You to do all the visioning in Your perfect
way." When a thing is left *entirely* in God's hands
He has complete power to work the greatest miracles
of healing.

This relinquishment involves the whole-hearted
acceptance of the Saving and Healing Christ. As we
turn to Christ in penitence and humility and gratitude for the blood He shed for mankind, we are
suddenly filled with a Life as boundless as the ocean,
as powerful as Niagara, and as loving and tender

and healing as the air we breathe. It was our sickness that he bore, our pains that he carried, he was pierced for our transgressions, he was bruised for our iniquities . . . and through his stripes we are healed.

EXERCISES FOR LESSON IV

READING EXERCISE: Read *How to Find Health Through Prayer.*

MEMORIZING EXERCISE: Memorize the 103rd Psalm.

VISUALIZATION EXERCISE: Use your imagination and witness Naaman's healing. Slowly he wades out into the Jordan. He feels the waters creeping higher and higher up his flesh, soothing the sore places, bringing life to the dead places. Up it creeps to his waist, then up to his shoulders, submerges his neck and then he closes his eyes and immerses his entire being, head and all, within its healing embrace.

Then he slowly walks out upon the shore, the bright sun-rays warming his head, his neck, his shoulders, his breast, and when he is completely emerged from the water he is completely submerged in the sunlight. Consider the beautiful partnership between these two—water and sunlight! There is no jealousy betwen them—only loving cooperation. Each relinquishes him gladly to the other.

As he turns toward the Jordan again the full force of the sun falls upon his back, the ultra-violet rays penetrating to every nerve and blood vessel the full length of the spine.

Having stood and basked awhile in the sun, again

he walks slowly into the healing waters. Then slowly out again. This he repeats seven times.

As he enters the Jordan each time his head is bowed in repentance and humility; as he emerges each time his head is uplifted to heaven in love and thanksgiving.

Now see yourself walking, not into water, but into the Jordan of God's purifying love, with head bowed in humility and repentance. Feel all the sins and errors of your life being washed away. Then walk out with love and faith and gratitude into the sunshine of God's Love and Gladness, letting His brightness permeate every pore of your being and every avenue of your soul.

Remember that Jesus promised you that if you "seek first the Kingdom of Heaven all these things will be added unto you." According to that promise, if this first bath—the bath of the soul—is taken completely enough, the cure will be accomplished without need of taking any of the other baths. That is true. Perhaps that is why John the Baptist did not repeat the seven-fold command of Elisha, but concentrated on the one bath, the bath of the soul, in the form of a baptism by water given by himself, followed by the baptism by the Spirit and by Fire given by Jesus Christ.

Because it is so difficult to achieve this perfect baptism of the soul, and because so few attain it in its perfection, at least in their first attempt, we shall proceed to the consideration of the other six baths. However, let me suggest that you turn back frequently to reread this chapter and hold it as central in all the healing process.

LESSON V

THE SECOND BATH: BATHING THE EMOTIONS

Dear friend:

This lesson carries you right down to the very roots where practically all human disease begins—the emotions.

There is a story of a Persian philosopher who came to a missionary with the request that he would read to him from the Bible every day, translating as he read. The first day the missionary read a passage that included the statement, "The tongue is a little member and boasteth great things." At that sentence he asked the reader to stop. A month went by. One day the missionary met him on the street and said, "I thought you were coming to have me read to you every day."

"It has taken me this long to get as much as you did read," was the reply. It may take you several weeks to complete this bath of the emotions.

It is in this lesson you may need special help. The usual custom is to turn to a trained psychiatrist. But there is a shorter way if you can turn to the One who created the psychiatrists, the One who created your emotions, the One who created the right solution for every problem.

When you are well along in this lesson or when you are near the end of it, you may wish to avail yourself of a great promise of Jesus "Where two or three agree together touching anything, in My name, it will be done." So if you wish to, feel free to write to the Prayer Tower, 1571 Grand Avenue, St. Paul 5, Minnesota, regarding your special need and let them "agree" with you in seeing it lifted.

Most people live in their emotions. This is the lesson that brings you right down to where you live. It may even take you down into the cellars of life. It is your one opportunity for a good stiff housecleaning. So get the ash man, the waste-paper man, the old-clothes man, the garbage man, all at work carting off the things you want

to get rid of, and have the plumber come in
with brand-new pipes and get you put into
perfect alignment with the Source of All
Life.

Sincerely yours,

Glenn Clark

THE SECOND BATH:
BATHING THE EMOTIONS

Diabetes is sometimes caused by self-condemnation. The "wasting away" of tuberculosis may be due to a subconscious desire to escape life. Allergies to certain life-giving foods have a similar origin. A young woman who came to my camps had an allergy to milk, tomatoes, and half a dozen other health-giving foods. She was very frail and doctors had not been able to help her. We asked her when the allergic condition originated and she recalled it was during a period of great discouragement when she actually wished to die. As she was speaking she suddenly remembered the occasion on which someone told her, with great emphasis, that these particular foods were very "life-giving." And then she recognized her subconscious motive in rejecting them. We asked, "Do you want to live now?" And she affirmed, "I most certainly do!" From that moment of affirmation all of her allergic tendencies vanished. In a few months she had regained her normal weight.

"Fully fifty per cent of the problems of the acute stages of an illness, and seventy-five per cent of the difficulties of convalescence, have their primary origin, not in the body, but in the mind of the patient," says Dr. Edward A. Strecker. In personal interviews Dr. Stanley Cobb, of Massachusetts General Hospital in Boston, discovered that ninety-six per cent of his patients showed serious resentments, seventy-five per cent were profoundly depressed, sixty-eight per cent were burdened with a deep sense of guilt. Dr. Leo Kanner says, "Physicians do not treat hearts, lungs, intestines, or kidneys lying between two bed sheets. They are now being taught to treat not only that which is sick but also him or her who is sick."

There is an ancient legend that man was free from death-dealing emotions until a foolish maiden named Pandora, consumed with curiosity, opened a box and all at once let out into the world a million pests. Now let us suppose she had released just two; and let us try to "swat" them. Dr. Horace Fletcher, from whose name the word "Fletcherize" was coined, made a great discovery that changed his whole life, and helped countless others in their efforts to make distinctions between virtue and vice. He found that Anger and Fear are the parents of all the vices, Anger of all the masculine vices, and Fear of all the feminine vices. Let us call them the two original pests. For instance, thrift is a virtue; but if thrift is "bitten" by the mosquito of Anger it becomes diseased into greed, and if it is "bitten" by Fear it becomes diseased into miserliness. Love infected with Anger becomes jealousy; love infected with Fear becomes envy. Inject these vices, even in small doses, into any virtue and the virtue becomes a vice. Conversely, any vice is instantly redeemed into a virtue when Fear and Anger are washed out with Faith and Love. These virtues are the very blood of life and flow freely from the heart of God, purifying and cleansing whenever we let them in.

And, so, bathing the emotions is a process of washing away Anger and Fear, and then soaking in

Love and Faith. It is easy to wash out Anger when we learn to dissociate vice from human intention. We do not become angry with a tubercular patient when he carries an active tubercular germ. We all carry these germs within us, but his is currently active. So why should we become angry with an irritable person, a jealous person, or a conceited person? We all carry these "germs" also, but his are currently active. We feel sorry for those who show symptoms of physical illness. Why not also feel sorry for those who suffer with sin? It may take some time to become adjusted to this concept but it can bring you health, vitality, release, and power without measure. Jesus, the Great Physician, used these methods which we are describing. When the Pharisees condemned him for seeking out the publicans and sinners, he replied, "I come not to the found, but to the lost, for they who are whole have no need of a physician." He seems to have been the first one who had the same compassion upon the sick and the sinful.

As Anger vanishes when we dissociate all evil from human intention, Fear vanishes when we turn to God. Thus, even evil with its consequent sorrows and suffering can serve the great purpose of driving us into the arms of God. As soon as we recognize this purpose, through a consciousness of our need, the evil itself will vanish, its work accomplished.

When a telephone bell rings continuously it may hurt our ears, but the noise is not the purpose of its ringing. The noise is merely a means to draw our attention to the receiver so that we may hear the message awaiting us at the other end of the line. As soon as we answer the ringing call, it ceases to annoy us, and instead of the noise, we now hear the message. When we accept every sickness, every trouble, every trial that comes to us as a call from God to listen for His message, we are not long disturbed by any of them and eventually learn to listen before He starts the "ringing." Let us beware of spiritual deafness!

God is the ruler over every phase of life, over the just and the unjust, the good and the bad, over sickness as well as health, and so there is nothing whatever to fear. It is only through union with God that we receive any permanent blessing. So death itself becomes the consummation of that most perfect union in which we forsake all fear and become one with all that our souls sincerely desire.

Evil can come to us only when we have separated ourselves at some point from the parent vine. "If a man abide not in me, he is cast forth as a branch, and is withered; and men gather them, and cast them into the fire, and they are burned." Separation creates a vacuum, and into a vacuum there flows any adjacent influence that can fill it. Unfortunately Fear is alway at the brink of spiritual vacuums; and Fear can fill them so completely that there is no room left for any other influence.

Fear is distrust of God's intentions, and thus blocks the cure that prayer could bring. For a vacuum when filled ceases to be a vacuum and cannot be refilled until it is emptied. It is only when we are utterly willing to relinquish ourselves and our loved ones to God that Fear pours out and leaves room for God to come in. If some hurt has been done

to us by another person our nearest emotion is likely
to be Anger or resentment. But when Anger flows
in, Joy and Love, the great overcomers, are blocked
out. The only way to empty out Anger is to forgive
our enemies. Forgiveness recreates the vacuum immediately, permitting God to enter in and answer
our prayers. "Father, forgive them, for they know
not what they do." Yes, Christ embodied forgiveness. But it is the forgiveness that passes understanding, for we must know that we are forgiven as
we show mercy to those who have hurt us. Now perfect Love casts out Fear, and so it brings us into the
perfect state of healing consciousness, in which even
death is known for what it is: "O grave where is thy
victory; O death, where is thy sting?"

Having emptied out evil thoughts of Anger and
Fear, and left room for God to come in, we will receive an inflowing of Love and Joy, moving as ir-
resistibly as air to fill a vacuum—as naturally as
water flowing downhill. When a radio set is properly
wired and properly tuned it will transform one kind of
energy into another. And so it is with prayer. When
we are properly "wired" with love and relinquishment and properly tuned to the wave-length of peace,
divine energy is transformed into atomic energy,
bringing healing out of the infinite into the finite
conditions of men. If you pray in love and trust and
discover that your anxiety is dissipating like a sum-
mer cloud you may believe your prayers are being
answered. If you pray with a group that is in harmony, and experience deep peace in their presence, it
is God's assurance that your prayer is being answered. If the peace becomes a sense of ecstasy, even

of bliss, you may know that a miracle is taking place in the mind and body of the one for whom you are praying. This is the peace that passeth understanding, that comes only after we have experienced the perfect purification of the baptism by water and received the perfect inspiration of the baptism by fire. Oh, that the world were filled with little prayer groups where harmony and devotion and experience of the presence of the living Christ were the regular routine of every day in every week!

EXERCISES FOR LESSON V

READING EXERCISE: *I Will Lift Up Mine Eyes,* chapters I and II. If you read two daily meditations each day you can cover this two weeks reading in one week.

MEMORIZING EXERCISE: Memorize the Psalm-Prayer of Harmony on page one hundred and nine of *The Soul's Sincere Desire.* If fear is one of your problems memorize this prayer, which you will find on page thirty-nine of *I Will Lift Up Mine Eyes:* "Our Heavenly Father, henceforth I shall have no fear, for I trust utterly in Thee, and Thou art the God of Love, giver of every good and perfect gift. Resting in Thee and abiding eternally in Thy love, I am impervious as in a citadel, for no evil can henceforth reach me without first passing through Thee, being transformed in the process into perfect purity, perfect harmony, and perfect love. Hold me close to Thy Heart, O Father, and accept my gratitude, my adoration, and my love. Amen."

VISUALIZATION EXERCISE: Hold in mind a person you dearly love and opposite him see someone who stands in need of love. Pour out a flood of love upon your dear one and then let that same love pour out upon the one in need of love.

Follow in your own way this exercise of which Mary Welch writes in *Reckoning at Dusk*.

"I drew up a plan for expressing love today in a special way. I listed the names of the first twelve loved persons entering my mind. These were persons for whom it is my natural disposition to pray daily with a spontaneous love. The names came faster than I could write. Then I started back at the top of the sheet of paper and beside each name I wrote another, a name that I consciously strove to find as being that of some person who might stand in need of more love in his or her life from somebody. These last names I paired with the first ones listed, thus giving to each loved person a "twin" for the day's experience of love and prayer.

"Then I started down the list in earnest prayer, dwelling on my full-hearted love for the first named one, rendering my gratitude for his or her place in my life, and giving that dear one to the Father for that day. Next I took the "twin" and lifted that one into the same realm of intense loving concern where I had effortlessly held the first one. I remained with each of my dozen sets of twins until each "twin" name had been raised to the same degree of warm ·love and had been prayed over with the same fervor as the first names had inspired. This was about as exciting a feat as I have ever attempted in my life. It required two hours of time and was certainly a soul-stretching exercise. Had I possessed any enemies to have paired with my great loves, their enmity should surely have been annihilated in this process. As I prayed, I felt a light burning within that made me know that at the very time something unusual was happening to those I used as 'twins.' "

THE THIRD BATH:
BATHING THE MIND

Dear friend:
Having bathed your soul and bathed your
emotions you are now ready to bathe your
mind. There are two ways to clear the mind:
one is to cast out old opinions, and the
other is to get new ones. In both cases the
process of doing this is to exercise the
mind.

So before the next lesson comes, take
time to review all the lessons that have
preceded this. Note, for instance, the great
emphasis I have been laying upon using the
imagination and visioning yourself as you
should be. The imagination is the queen of
the intellectual faculties. It is the power
that lifts a man from mediocrity to genius.
Few people realize that by the same law,
imagination may lift a person from illness
to health and from frailty to strength.

For several weeks now your imagination
has been given some training in relaxing
your body and releasing your tensions. In
all those exercises while you were relaxing
your imagination, at the same time, on a
deeper level, you were relaxing your soul.

But lest your imagination become too
relaxed and too lazy, it has been given some
good stiff jobs of memorizing. Only those
with good imaginations remember well. Imaginative children recall events clear back
to their second year. The rest of us common
folk do well to go back to our fourth year.

The intellect is the work horse in this
course. It fetches and carries. It is when
the intellect relaxes itself out of the picture and lets the All-Mind take charge in
its Spaceless, Timeless way, that a vast
sense of peace and a high realization of
perfect happiness and perfect health flows
in.

Let your mind mark passages that mean
the most to you, let your memory recall
them, let your imagination see the real,
whole person where others see limitations,
and then using the mind as a springboard,
leap off into great silent spaces and get

still in the recognition that God is ever present, and that His wholeness wraps you round.

When you have finished all the exercises in this lesson, turn back and reread this letter.

Sincerely yours,

Glenn Clark

THE THIRD BATH:
BATHING THE MIND

The bathing of the Mind, just as the bath of the Soul and the bath of the Emotions, has two phases: the cleansing out of the wrong ideas by the bath of water, and the drawing in of the right ideas by the bath of the spirit.

For convenience's sake I am going to divide this theme into three phases: one, the sponge bath; two, the shower bath; three, the tub bath.

I. THE SPONGE BATH

By this I mean the careful sponging out from your mind of all its old unnecessary opinions. It is all right to have your attic filled up with old books that you never read, old clothes that you never wear, and old trinkets that you never will care to look at again. Of course some day these things will have to be cleared away, probably by some overworked, harassed daughter after you have gone to your heavenly reward. It is all right to let the dust accumulate on the shelves and floor of this attic that you never go into. But to have your mind, which God intended to be a spic-and-span workroom for you to live in and use every day, all cluttered up with useless junk which is of no value excepting to accumulate dust, is one of the worst errors you could commit. There is nothing that will bring you wrinkles and make your hair turn grey faster than to live and work in such surroundings.

What are the unnecessary opinions that should be thrown into the junk heap? One thing you can be sure of is that any negative opinion always belongs in this list. If that negative opinion is about someone else, you can eradicate it most easily by putting it through this test: first, is it true; second, is it kind; third, is it necessary? Then cast out the opinion and sponge out all the dust and debris accumulated around it with a prayer of healing. If the negative opinion is about yourself, put it through this test: first, is it true of you as a son of God, not as the mean little runt you think you are? Second, does it express real faith and respect for the One who made you—your Divine Creator? If it doesn't meet these tests cast it out, purify the space it formerly occupied in your consciousness with a prayer, and in its place establish a hobby. A hobby is a fine, clear window pane that lets the light of God in. If every room could exchange its old, dusty shutters for brand new window panes, smiles would take the place of wrinkles and health would take the place of disease.

This scrubbing out of the mind of all its old negatives is the sponge bath. When you have sponged out these old opinions and habits, the bath with water has been completed. If you want to carry the metaphor further, you can now take a perfectly clean sponge and dip it in some precious oil that is sun-kissed and vitamin-bearing, that is commonly known as hobbies. There is nothing that will freshen up a tired-out mind as some activity like gardening, golfing, fishing, sculpturing, painting, and the tinkering one can do with pieces of wood and a tool chest.

II. THE SHOWER BATH

What do we mean by the shower bath?

There's nothing that will tire a thinker so quickly as the feeling that he does all the thinking himself. The moment he catches the spirit of Joel Chandler Harris who learned how to let the "Other Fellow" lean over his shoulder and do the writing through him, or the secret of George Eliot, who let the "Other Self" do her writing, the wear and tear on the thinking process is greatly lessened. The baptism by fire was symbolized in the experience of Isaiah by the touching of the coal to his lips. That immediately converted his human brain from being a "factory" *manufacturing* ideas into a "channel" for bringing *ideas into birth*. If one can keep in alignment, and tune into the Infinite, the right thoughts will come in perfect sequence and in perfect order, just the right ideas at the right time to bring peace, inspiration, happiness, and comfort to those whom he is with.

The shower bath I am referring to is nothing more or less than stepping into the stream of God-consciousness and having confidence that, while you may have certain responsibilities in adjusting the stream and regulating the temperature and directing its flow, nevertheless the stream itself comes from a Power greater than you. The way to step into the stream and put yourself into alignment is to follow two rules. First, tune one ear in to the voice of God, trusting that He will send you the right ideas you need; and second, tune your other ear into the needs in the hearts of men and be responsive to the pull they put upon you. Open your soul to the living fountain which is constantly pouring a perfect, fresh set of ideas into you, and open your heart to those about you, as to a living vortex that is constantly drawing the right ideas out of you. Take freely all that God sends you and give freely to your friends all you have. This will take all strain out of your thinking. Your mind will work with ease as never before.

If you have already taken the sponge bath and have washed away the encrusted opinions that were clinging to you, this second bath of stepping into the living flow of life-giving ideas will have a marvelous healing effect upon your mind and body. From now on whenever you are called upon to give a spiritual talk remember to step into this living stream and you will be more rested when you finish than when you began.

III. The Tub Bath

For this bath you will need a very large tub; in fact, for the complete healing effect I wish to describe, it should be a veritable swimming pool. For I want you to immerse your entire being in it. Just as in a former lesson you were taught to see everything as wholes and not as fragments, so now you are to immerse your whole mind in God, and not a mere part of it. Our education, our business, in fact nearly everything we do has divided us up into so many compartments that it is a positive wonder that we are not all split personalities.

Anything which is whole is beautiful. A whole tree is something to write a poem about, but when sawed up into a lumber pile it will not inspire any poem. A whole rabbit or a whole sheep is beautiful, but when hanging in the butcher shop there is something lost. There is life in a whole tree and in a whole rabbit and in a whole sheep, but when these things are divided into fragments the life is lost.

So I recommend that you form the habit of seeing every idea as a unified truth integrated in proper relationship with other truths. See every event as an expression of the wholeness of life in its proper relationship with the other events. And, above all, see every person you meet as a unified, total personality in perfectly adjusted and harmonious relationship with all other persons and with God. There is nothing that will make you a perfect being in a perfect world, governed by a perfect God as quickly as forming the habit of seeing everyone else as a perfect being also. There is nothing that will make you a whole person so permanently as this habit of seeing wholeness in others. When you find yourself becoming split up into fragmentariness and dis-ease, go back to your pool of wholeness and take a good long dip in the tub.

I. When you have learned how to make use of the sponge bath and have sponged away the old opinions, you will find yourself growing young again.

II. When you have become a channel thinker instead of a factory thinker, you will find fatigue vanishing from your life and genius coming in.

III. When you have immersed yourself in wholeness until you can see everyone as whole, you will find yourself becoming whole, and bringing wholeness to others.

EXERCISES FOR LESSON VI

READING EXERCISE. Read Chapters III, IV and V of *I Will Lift Up Mine Eyes*. Concentrate on "Climbing the Stairways" in Lesson III. It truly requires a clearing of the mind merely to hit the right note in the scale of the full realization of the *meaning* of the words. This week's exercise will constitute a truly invigorating bath of the mind.

MEMORIZING EXERCISE: Review all the memorized passages of the past four weeks.

MIND RELAXING EXERCISE: Shake yourself out of ruts as completely as you can for the next week. Try any new thing that you think will interest you.

Get crayons and start drawing,

or

Get paints and start painting,

or

Get tools and start handicraft,

or

Crochet or rug-weave.

Go to the city library and browse among many magazines you have not seen.

Better still, browse among many books you never read before. Find some line or several lines you would really like to follow further and take home several books to read.

THE FOURTH BATH:
BATHING THE LUNGS

Dear friend:

In this lesson for the first time in this course we step down into the physical. Having bathed the soul, mind, and emotions we consider now the bathing of the lungs.

It is essential to our purpose that we feel no jar in this transition, and we need not if we are as skilled in matters of the Spirit as air pilots are who bring their planes into perfect landings without their passengers knowing when the wheels touch the earth.

There is no better analogy for practicing the living presence of God than the air we breathe. Air is invisible; so is God.

Who hath seen the wind?
Neither you nor I;
But when the trees bow down their heads
The wind is passing by.

Who hath seen our God?
Neither you nor I;
But when strong men bow down their heads
Then God is passing by.

Air is in us and we are in the air: God is in us and we are in God. We couldn't escape Him if we would and we wouldn't if we could. It is only through the air that we can communicate one with another; and it is only through God that we can reach the souls of each other. Through the air a speaker for the radio can reach thousands at the same time. God, through the mysteries of His Spiritual "ozone" can speak to everyone in the whole world at the same time.

The word Spirit means breath, yes the very air we breathe. So think of the exercises of this lesson as nothing more or less than a real communion with God through the the medium of the Spirit.

Sincerely yours,

Glenn Clark

THE FOURTH BATH:
BATHING THE LUNGS

"As the hart panted after the water brooks, so panted my soul after Thee, O God."

The bath of the lungs can be especially healing if it be made an instrument through which can flow the three higher baths that have preceded it. If while our body is breathing in the air of this outer world our soul is breathing in the air of the inner world, the effect will be tremendously invigorating.

"Just as the body dies if it has no air to breathe," writes Henry Thomas Hamblin, "and the mind also ceases to function if it has no atmosphere which it can breathe, so also the soul is starved and suffocated if it cannot breathe what Carpenter termed 'the sweet ethers blowing of the breath of God.' Although we cannot remember it, no doubt, when we were children, we breathed naturally and freely of the true atmosphere of the soul. This probably continued so long as we remained simple, artless, gentle, and kind. Jesus said 'Whosoever shall not receive the Kingdom of God as a little child, he shall not enter therein.'

"We see, therefore, that we have to be born again, or become as little children, and breathe once again the finer ethers of the Spirit, in order that we may enter the Kingdom of God and become conscious sons of God. But as we grow older we become separated from finer and inner worlds through the growth of a hard shell of egoism. The soul became starved, because it was not allowed to breathe. Thus we became what is termed spiritually dead."

But how can one "breathe" spiritually one may ask. To this Mr. Hamblin continues:

"Sending out our love to mankind; pouring out our soul upon all peoples and created things; emptying ourselves in a passionate attempt to bless others; all these tend to set the inner breathing going."

Let us follow Mr. Hamblin a little further in his illuminating discoveries:

"As we go deeper and deeper, we realize that there is That within us which is eternal; and that this deep interior breathing, which we experience, goes right down to the Centre of Being.

"Those of us who have not yet reached this stage can take comfort from the fact that love is the key, always. If we love and if we are kind, then our soul is given some of the breath of Heaven. If we praise and adore the Author and Centre of our being, again our soul is given an opportunity to breathe the Heavenly atmosphere.

"Every time that we turn to God; every time that we become quiet in Him; every time that we stay our haste; every time that we follow the teaching of Jesus our soul is let out of prison to a certain extent, and allowed to breathe the Spiritual atmosphere.

"First of all we have to empty our soul. If we do this, God will fill it. Thus we become spiritually alive through our soul breathing the atmosphere of God.

"Nothing can satisfy this deep longing and hunger of the soul but the actual breathing of its own natural atmosphere—the breath of God."

"With each Divine impulse," says Emerson in *The Oversoul*, "soul rends the thin rind of the visible and finite, and comes out into eternity and *inspires* and *expires* its air."

I can carry this illustration further by turning to my own *Soul's Sincere Desire* * in which I wrote:

"There is nothing that clears the brain and avenues of circulation like breathing with eleven-elevenths of the lungs and not with one-eleventh—breathing out the old waste poisons and breathing in the new clear life from the atmosphere which surrounds us. We should pray out the bad and pray in the good; dismiss from our minds the trouble which seems imminent and restate emphatically the great promises of God; forgive the sinner and accept forgiveness for the sin.

"Before it is possible to breathe, one must be surrounded by atmosphere and atmosphere must *be in one.* Likewise, before it is possible to commune with God, which is a more conventional way of characterizing the deep breathing of the soul, one must know that God surrounds all and God is in all; that the Kingdom of Heaven is *here* and *now.*

"As breathing is a mere rhythmic interchange of that which is within for that which is without, a casting-out of that which seems to be bad and a receiving, in its stead, of that which seems to be good, so the breathing of the soul is a casting-out of all that would poison, cramp or belittle life—in short all that is *unlike* God, and a taking-in of all that is pure, perfect, and joyous, and which enriches life—in short, that which is *like* God.

"And just as in physical breathing we give a quick expulsion of the poisons we wish to eliminate, and then drink in slowly of the new, fresh, life-giving, body-building ozone, holding it, first deep in the lungs, then high, turning it over, so to speak, till we have completely absorbed the life-giving oxygen, so we should give our denials with expulsive force, turning instantly to the constructive soul-

* *The Soul's Sincere Desire,* Glenn Clark, Little, Brown & Co., Boston. $2.00

building affirmations. The trouble with most of our praying, as with our breathing, is that it is too negative. We shut ourselves up in a cramped little three-dimensional room with our negations, breathing in again and again the troubles that we should let vanish into thin air, instead of turning to new and fresh air—to God.

"Marvelous results will come if one will turn in thought to God and Heaven, deny the existence in Heaven of the wrong thing felt or thought, and then realize that in God and Heaven the opposite condition prevails. One must dismiss from his mind completely the thought that the wrong thing felt or seen is permanent, and then follow instantly with the realization that the opposite condition exists here and now."

Here is a splendid breathing exercise for the soul, taken from my book, *The Way, the Truth and the Life.** On the left is the out-breathing of the bad, and on the right is the in-breathing of the good. We can call it:

A Psalm of Healing

The Lord is my Shepherd:	For He maketh me to lie down in green pastures.
I shall not want for peace:	
I shall not want for serenity:	For He leadeth me beside the still waters.
I shall not want for healing:	For He restoreth my soul.
I shall not want for guidance:	For He leadeth me in paths of righteousness, for His name's sake.
The Lord is My Shepherd:	For Thou art with me in the valley and the shadow.
I shall fear no evil from death:	

* *The Way, the Truth and the Life,* Glenn Clark, Harper, New York. $2.00

I shall fear no evil from danger:	For Thy rod and Thy staff shall protect me.
I shall fear no evil from famine:	For Thou preparest a table before me in the presence of mine enemies.
I shall fear no evil from mental disturbances:	For Thou annointest my head with oil.
I shall fear no evil from want:	For my cup runneth over.
I shall fear no evil from sin:	For goodness and mercy shall follow me all the days of my life.
I shall fear no evil from separation from my Heavenly Father:	For I shall dwell in the house of the Lord forever.

Few people know how to breathe properly. Ordinarily you breathe out sixteen quarts of carbon dioxide every hour. This is necessary merely to live. But with this kind of breathing your body is also slowly dying. When you reach the age of seventy or eighty you will be quite old. Now if for one hour you breathe out fifteen quarts instead of sixteen quarts you will feel depleted in direct proportion to this lack. On the contrary, if you breathe out even a little more than sixteen quarts your body will be rejuvenated remarkably. And if—as you breathe physiologically—your mind and soul cooperate with high spiritual thinking and pure outgoing love, the results will be remarkable.

To learn how to breathe perfectly, watch a little child sleeping. He takes a deep breath, then immediately exhales, relaxing so completely as he exhales that he has no impulse to inhale again for several full seconds. The only time when the heart and lungs—the most overworked organs of the entire body—can get a complete rest is during those few seconds between each breath when there is no oxygen in the lungs to work upon. And if you could always breathe as a sleeping child breathes, your heart might keep running for a hundred and twenty years.

Watch a dog as it follows you on a stroll down the street. It does not breathe; it pants. Take a little vigorous exercise, and you too will be panting. And how do you breathe when panting? As a little child does when he is sleeping, only a little more vigorously. Each ingoing breath will be shorter than usual; each outgoing breath will be longer. There will be no pause between the ingoing and outgoing breaths, but there will be a pause after every outgoing breath.

This is breathing which revives and resurrects life if it is accompanied with joyous, loving thoughts. If you will take twelve or fifteen minutes a day for some happy, contemplative breathing "thy youth shall be renewed like the eagle's."

I have given you the simple method of learning how to breathe. Now we will explore a more complex method. Take a deep breath but do not raise the chest or clavicle. Rather, flare your ribs, pulling in the abdomen. As you exhale place your hands on your ribs, pressing in until the lungs are emptied. Inhale again, with your hand over the stomach. Feel it expand as the ribs flare apart. At the same time your abdominal muscles will be pulling the abdomen in toward your back. Now exhale, pressing your hands against your ribs until they are emptied. The stomach area is relaxed. All exercises should be done rhythmically; especially is it necessary to breathe in a rhythmic cycle. As you inhale count to five; hold your breath to a count of two; exhale to a count of five.

Now lie down on your back, shoulders pressed against the floor, and try these breathing exercises:

1. Inhale to a count of five, following above instructions. Hold to a count of two. Then exhale to a count of five, completely relaxing the abdominal muscles. Rest to a count of two, and then repeat. Do this ten to twelve times.

2. Using the same count inhale while you raise both legs together, bending at the knees until the upper legs hug the body. Now, holding your breath to a count of two, unbend the knees and raise the legs, pushing them up at right angles to the body. As you exhale to a count of five lower the legs without bending the knees, keeping the toes pointed, and rest again on the floor. Do this twelve times.

3. Inhaling to a count of five raise your arms from the floor in an arc over your head until they touch the floor above your head. Do not stiffen the arms as you lift them. Now, to a count of three or four reach your arms above your head so as to stretch the entire body from the pelvic region. Then expel the breath in one rapid exhalation, returning the arms in an arc to rest again at your sides. While you were stretching upward your lungs were full thus pressing the diaphragm against the abdominal organs. The sudden release from this position gives a vital kick to the diaphragm. Repeat twelve times.

4. The next time you go out into the open air try

inhaling a complete breath in sniffs, as smelling aromatics. Do not exhale between those whiffs until the entire lung space is filled. Retain a few seconds. Then exhale in a long, restful, sighing breath through the nostrils.

When you take a walk in the open air on a country lane or bypath run about ten paces every twenty-five yards and pant naturally after each run.

Games in the open air with friendly competition in them are especially valuable for washing out the lungs. The fun with which you play the game adds healing quality to the breath you draw. But simple walking can be one of the best exercises of all, when done with the body and head erect, and breathing properly and with happy thoughts in the mind.

One final note before closing this lesson. We take many poisons into our bodies through the stomach but there is one poison which millions of Americans imbibe through their lungs every day. This is nicotine. Since normal breathing is a process of inhaling the good and casting out the bad, smokers exactly reverse this process, nullifying its chief values. Most deaths due to coronary thrombosis occur among heavy smokers. Records now show that the increase in lung cancer keeps pace with the increase in cigarette smoking.

Smokers claim that cigarettes give them a "lift." Actually it is a temporary stimulation, created by the release of epinephrine from the adrenal glands which are attempting to combat the poisons affecting the heart when the lungs take in nicotine. It is obvious that bathing the lungs is no cure for an evil that involves continual reinfection. The root lies deep in the mind and emotions, and bathing should begin there.

EXERCISES FOR LESSON VII

READING EXERCISE: Read *Recovery* by Starr Daily.

MEMORIZING EXERCISE: Memorize the adaptation of the 23rd Psalm on page sixty-seven and repeat it every day for a week silently while using some of the breathing exercises discussed in this lesson.

MEDITATION EXERCISE: Meditate on portions of the last chapter in any of these books: *Thought Farthest Out, Soul's Sincere Desire* or *I Will Lift Up Mine Eyes*. There is a lot of "fresh air" in all of these chapters.

THE FIFTH BATH:
BATHING THE BLOOD VESSELS

Dear friend:

I wish you joy for this week!

The spiritual significance of the veins and arteries are channels in consciousness, and the spiritual significance of blood is the joy that flows through these channels in consciousness. There is positively nothing more health-giving than joy. Joy propelled by love is the medicine that no disease can stand before. Germs, infections, rheumatism, ulcers—all vanish away before the healthy flow of joy-filled blood propelled by a heart of love.

Saturate yourself with this thought morning, noon, and night by memorizing the Psalm-Prayer of Joy in The Soul's Sincere Desire, and repeating it often. Set it to music and sing it if you want to.

What stimulates the blood to flowing most vigorously is the movements of the muscles. Spiritually speaking, the muscles are nothing but the externalizing of our thought-forces. Every thought you think is registered in your muscles. You think a thought of fear or anger and it tenses some muscle; if it is a severe thought it tenses all your muscles. Tensed muscles interfere with the easy natural flow of the circulation. Keep on tensing them and they pull the spine out of alignment. When the spine gets out of alignment the vertebra pinch upon nerves that control various body functions. An osteopath or chiropractor may get the spine back in alignment but if you keep up your wrong thinking your thought-forces will pull it right out again.

Therefore, relax your muscles and at the same time let go of your angers and fears and other mental and emotional tensions. Then as you stretch and swing yourself into normal, healthy, muscular exercises, the life-giving emotions of love and joy will go swinging through your consciousness.

A book that will help you do this better than anything I can think of next to

The Secret Garden is The Healing Light by
Agnes Sanford. The joyful optimism and loving human atmosphere it carries makes it the
perfect book for you to read at this stage
of this healing course. In my Foreword to
the book I say that it creates the ideal
"healing climate." As you complete the reading of that book this week think of yourself
as living, moving, and having your being in
a healing climate. Saturate yourself in this
healing climate as you read.

Now remember--the prescription for this
lesson is love and joy--and especially
plenty of joy. Not only feel joy, but consciously think joy. Let joy get into your
"thought-forces"--in other words, into your
whole muscular system. Think joy, speak joy,
act joy. Let joy sit with you at your meals.
Let joy be the last thing you think of at
night and the first thing you think of in
the morning. Obey Shakespeare's injunction,
"Let joy be unconfined." And, above all,
remember what Jesus said, "These things have
I spoken unto you that my joy might remain
in you, and that your joy might be full."

Sincerely yours,

Glenn Clark

THE FIFTH BATH:
BATHING THE BLOOD VESSELS

In the last lesson we discovered that it is not work or food that age one's body, but impurities. During that last lesson, whether you knew it or not, your lungs were breathing out 34,400 quarts of impure air every day. For the next lesson following this one you will find that your intestines and kidneys are carrying off quarts of waste every day. In the tenth lesson, you will find that the skin is squeezing out impurities through 2,000,000 little tubes. In this way God and nature are working for you every hour. They keep these processes active even when you do not give them a chance.

What part does your blood play in this purifying process? Your blood is the living fluid of life. The mystics spoke truly when they called it the "living blood of the lamb of God." It rushes through your body, quarts of it every minute, purifying every cell.

When it comes to the bath of the blood vessels the most effective way to stimulate the flow of blood is through the exercises of the muscles. The more responsive to the Spirit we can make the muscles, the more healing will be the bathing of the circulatory system.

Your muscles may be strong, yet no more responsive than a stick of wood. Or they may be weak and about as responsive as a dishrag. To you they have been just muscles—hard and stiff or soft and flabby.

But now with your clearer vision you want them to be as responsive to Spirit as the ocean is to the pull of the moon, as powerful as the sea-waves when you need such power, and as gentle as the ripples on a quiet lake in the moonlight.

This problem of the responsiveness of your muscles is vitally important! To make them responsive you must learn how to tense them and how to relax them, physically, mentally, and spiritually. Let me tell you how to spiritualize the activity of your muscles.

Your muscles form three-fourths of your entire body and are your *means of expression* here on earth. You cannot even speak except by action of the muscles of your throat, cheeks, tongue, and lips. Every expression of your face, every body movement, is due to *muscle* movement. You cannot look at anything, unless little muscles move your eyeballs.

Hence, it is *very* important that you *spiritualize* the activity of your muscles *if* you want Spirit in you to express fully and completely.

Yet all your life your thoughts have been so materialistic that you have been *tensing* your muscles and *blocking up* energy; and as a result, you are often so tired you have no impulse to express anything.

To heighten muscular responsiveness our first lesson should be a lesson in physical relaxation. So lie down now, comfortably, and command each portion of your body to relax. If you have arthritis in the back begin there, and say: "Spine, be relaxed." If you have indigestion begin with the stomach, and say: "Stomach, be relaxed." And so on over the whole body, limb by limb and joint by joint. Wait a bit after each command until you feel the full response, and be very patient with the parts of the body which have suffered most from your tensions. They may tense up again before you are through with the rest of the body. Just repeat the command to them, and they will again obey.

Muriel Lester in an article entitled "The Prayer of Relaxation" told of a girl who was ill for seven or eight months with an over-strained heart, and was told she would never get cured because of her temperament: she enjoyed everything too much. This was a challenge to the foundation of her faith and the basis of her philosophy. Was it not God's will that one should enjoy all His gifts to the full. After much thought, she evolved a plan, the result of which was that she was back at work in a month, cured. It took her one hour a day for a month to get the cure. She would let nothing interfere with that hour. She had been ill a long time. The nerves of her heart had struck work apparently. Her breathing was irregular and jerky; her heart would miss a beat and then race like an engine. If she was interested in anything her toes curled up inside her shoes, her fingers tightened up as though her hand was clenched. If she was reading, her face muscles became tense. Whenever she was doing anything she was physically strung up.

Now, all those habits had to be undone; every muscle had to relax and become accustomed to a state of relaxation. That state had to be realized as a normal state, what God wills for one. She had been living on her nerves for a year or so without knowing it due to a series of calamities which had battered upon her family.

She told of how she felt like a piece of overstrung elastic, or yesterday's lettuce. The elastic could not regain its resilience, but the lettuce could recover its vigor if it was plunged into water. And she knew she could recover her freshness, both physically and spiritually, as soon as she became receptive to the all-pervading power of God. So for an hour each day she set herself the definite task of regaining renewal of vitality from God through relaxation.

She stretched herself out on her back, her weight concentrated on the nerve center at the back of her waist. Then she relaxed her muscles and spread them out as though they were the model for an artist—made her whole arm relaxed—then the same with the toes and the feet— then, a much harder task, with the face muscles. She discovered that to smile automatically relaxes all the face muscles and rests the nerves.

When she got to the face muscles she found the hand and finger muscles all taut again, and she had to begin the relaxing process all over. It took perhaps fifteen minutes to get really relaxed all over.

After she relaxed she listened to her own breathing, noticing how regular it had become, and as she listened it became slower. Then she suddenly realized how tired she was. Previously she had felt energetic and tireless because of her over-stimulated, ill-regulated nerves. But with relaxation the artificial stimulus was withdrawn, and the nerves were recovering their tone. Gradually the tiredness was transformed into deep restfulness. With her mind she kept saying, "With every breath I draw I am breathing in the breath of God," and peace seemed to envelop her whole being.

After a time she became possessed of all the strength and vigor she needed, and she began to use the last twenty minutes of the hour for others. Slowly and deliberately she thought of her friends, enemies, celebrities, public men in positions of great responsibility, and many others, young and old. As she thought of each of these she prayed,

"Breathe on them Breath of God; fill them with life anew; that they may love what Thou dost love, and do what Thou wouldst do." In telling her story she said, "These prayers reminded me of the process by which a photographic film is put into a printing frame and exposed to the light. One does not argue or wonder about the probability of the sensitised paper taking the impression from the film. One knows that when the frame is opened the print will be clear, and it is. The contrast between my feelings before and after the hour's prayer reminded me of the familiar experience on a July day in a garden. The flower beds are parched, pale and dry with heat, quite prickly if one touches them. A sudden shower comes and not only is the ground a rich brown once more and soft to the touch, but it exudes a refreshing odor."

Here is a form of breathing that may help you to relax as this girl relaxed.

As you breathe, do so to the rhythm of the following concepts. Think the words without speaking them.

"I am breathing out old, monotonous memories; I am breathing in new ideas."

"I am breathing out old prejudices; I am breathing in new truths."

"I am breathing out old fears; I am breathing in new courage."

"I am breathing out old jealousies; I am breathing in new love."

"I am breathing out old resentments; I am breathing in new forgiveness."

"I am breathing out old sorrows; I am breathing in new gladness."

"I am breathing out old remorses; I am breathing in new absolution."

"I am breathing out old obsessions; I am breathing in new freedom."

"I am breathing out love to all the world; I am breathing in the life and love of God."

Four words can consummate this period of spiritual relaxation. Breath in each capitalized word; let it linger on your lips. Taste it, feel it. Then breathe out, letting the slogan that follows the first word trail off silently. Repeat this series a half dozen times.

RELAXATION: The secret of a quiet body. . . .
TRANQUILITY: The secret of a quiet mind. . . .
SERENITY: The secret of a quiet soul . . . and
PEACE: The gift of God.

When you have completed these exercises for relaxing the muscles of your lungs we are going to start exercising the muscles of the outer body.

I. When one is still in bed in the morning one of the most health-building exercises is to stretch and twist just as a cat when it starts the day. After stretching one's arms and legs, one should roll and twist and writhe until every sinew and joint is limbered and glowing with new life. You will feel like a machine that has been well oiled.

II. Arise from your bed and stand erect, taking a wide stance. Bend sideways collapsing at the waist, flopping over to one side like a rag doll. Be completely relaxed with the head and arms dangling. Now roll forward from the waist and let the arms swing like pendulums, fingertips close to the floor.

Then roll from one side to the other side, arms dangling. Now pull yourself erect lifting the arms first horizontally stretching every portion of the body. Then bend forward all relaxed shaking your arms and shoulders as though dropping out old ideas. Rise again and stretch upward arms toward the sun, and welcome a new day.

III. Stand erect. Let the head and torso fall forward until the fingertips come close to the floor and every vertebra in the back is relaxed. With the head still hanging, and neck relaxed, rise slowly pulling from the base of the spine, then the middle, and last of all from the back of the neck until the head comes up erect. Now stand as though a string is attached to the top of your head, pulling you up and drawing your spine into perfect alignment. Repeat this exercise; it can actually increase your height.

IV. To the lilting music of a radio or phonograph dance about the room with swinging, upward motions of gratitude and joy. Throw your arms up high. When you have had enough, lean over and pick up armloads of LOVE and toss out blessings to the east and west, the north and south—to all your fellowmen.

V. These exercises will do much toward making your muscles responsive, radio-like, to the Spirit. If you love long walks, try taking a Three Mile Walk with God.

The first mile should be dedicated to relaxation of mind. Let your mind become blank so far as possible. Concentrate on the breathing concepts we have given in this and in the last chapter. Get still with the stillness of complete surrender. This is your chance to swing in perfect rhythm with the universe! Look up at the sky, out at the world, and be conscious of the solid undergirding of the earth.

The second mile should be dedicated to recuperation. Feel the thrill of new life flowing through your veins, drink deeply—not only of air but of space. Dwell on the ideas that come naturally and gladly to the mind, and only those. Feel love and joy flowing through your responsive muscles at every step.

The third mile is to be dedicated to inspiration. As you start it, turn upward in joy to God and outward in love to men. Open all the windows of your soul expectantly to receive the inspired ideas God will send to you. Having made your mind a blank for the first mile, a sponge for absorbing sunshine and happiness for the second, let it now become a radiant channel for the third. Do not judge or check any concepts as they come to you in this third mile. For now God will begin to reveal the pattern of your life in the full terms of His divine plan. When you reach home you will know He is truly "closer than breathing and nearer than hands and feet."

My secretary, Mrs. Glen Stowe, doesn't have time for a three mile walk so she has outlined a very effective "Seven Block Walk":

"A fifteen-minute walk to work or home from work can be of great value. All one needs is seven good-sized blocks to make this very effective. Block after block can be a going somewhere spiritually as well as physically.

"The first block. Cast aside every atom of personality. Begin your spiritual walk by centering your thoughts on

God with this mental statement, NOTHING MATTERS BUT GOD. Blank out all personalities and experiences, your own most of all.

"The second block is RECOGNITION AND RELATIONSHIP. Know the power of God. Recall some incident where, when all human effort failed, God walked in and straightened out the tangle. Know the continual awareness of God, the love, wisdom, and tenderness of God. Let thoughts of these attributes develop as you walk this block. This is very important and requires concentration. Then pass to establishing your relationship with God. You are made in the image and likeness of Him. If you believe this then you have in some degree the power of God, the knowledge of God, the love and wisdom of God. You have the power to control your thought. You have the knowledge of God which gives you skill for your work. A very important fact follows this; IF YOU RECOGNIZE THIS POWER AND KNOWLEDGE AND CONSCIOUSLY RELATE YOURSELF TO IT THEN YOUR ABILITIES AND YOUR SKILL INCREASE. You have the love of God which causes you to stoop to life and hold someone who has fallen and care for him until help comes and feel a great warmth of love for that person which surges in waves through you and blankets you both. You have the wisdom of God to guard your speech and guide your judgments.

"The third block. Here work really begins. This is the block of Love. Here you take your capacity to love and enlarge it. Close off everything from your mind but the one word Love. Start with that. See it in high letters. LOVE. Then feel it—the most powerful thing in the world, LOVE, its over-allness, its closeness, its permeating, penetrating quality. Now think of a person for whom you feel a great divine passion of tenderness and devotion—Jesus, if you are ready for Him, otherwise someone who reflects Jesus to you. Feel the warmth of that kindled flame and then focus it to include someone or some group that you find it difficult to love. You can get a good workout here for the best and highest that is in you.

"The fourth block. Now you are ready for adventure, the adventure of FAITH, and since this block takes you past the great cathedral you call it the FAITH BLOCK. You know as you enter here that with God as your guide you will surely reach the other end of this city block. You begin there and nothing moves you from that stand. Your faith is like rock, unyielding; You know you will arrive. Now stretch your faith a little to include the remainder of the walk, then through the next hour and the rest of the day; and from here on ANYTHING CAN HAPPEN ACCORDING TO YOUR FAITH.

"The fifth block. This is the Taking and Giving stretch. Take all of the rich gifts your Father gives you. Claim all of the things that He has promised you, such as safety, protection, guidance, and substance. Consciously accept these riches and then with joyful and reckless abandon give everything back to God. Give Him your personality, your thoughts, your love, your desires, your life. Just hand them all over into His extended hands and know the supreme bliss of belonging to someone else, of knowing no responsibility, no will but His, with the "government being on His shoulders," and you go FREE.

"The sixth block. This is the block of Gratitude and Consecration. Acknowledge and be thankful for the ability to hear the birds, to see and to behold the firmament, for feet that carry you, for hands, for health. Be thankful for life itself, for work, for God's abundance with which He has blessed you, and at the end of this block Rejoice and Be Glad. Those words appear so many times in the Bible that they must be important. They are healing and health giving.

"The seventh and last block. This is the block of Quiet.

Relax and rest in the peace of the walk. Be quiet in the shelter of your deepened awareness and quickened perceptions, just feeling and abiding in all of God's goodness, and knowing peace at having walked with Him."

EXERCISES FOR LESSON VIII

READING EXERCISE: Read Agnes Sanford's *Healing Light*.

MEDITATION EXERCISE I: Do some of the relaxing, breathing, and stretching exercises described in this lesson.

MEDITATION EXERCISE II: Take the three mile walk. If this is too far try the Seven Block Walk.

THE SIXTH BATH:
BATHING THE INNER TISSUES

Dear friend:

Our Study Course began with the symbolical significance of the two healing instruments of God, sunshine and water. We found that they represented Love and Joy on the one hand, and Humility and Trust on the other. The four men who lifted up the paralytic and let him down through the tiled roof into the very presence of Jesus might very well have been those four traits: Faith, Hope, Love, and Humility.

But now that we come to the actual use of water and sunshine, don't forget their real, that is, their spiritual meaning. Sometimes the real meaning of a thing is more real than the actual (material) meaning, if you get what I mean!

At the Last Supper Jesus took the juice of the grape and the unleavened whole-wheat wafer and said something like this, "When you drink this cup you are not drinking grape juice, you are drinking the life-giving elements of the Christ in me. When you are eating this bread you are assimilating the spiritual, life-giving vitamins of all that I represent. I am taking my body out of this world; so from now on the only bodies I shall have here to carry messages and do my work for me will be your bodies. I want those bodies to be marvelously strong and vital and capable of infinite service for the Kingdom. Therefore take this cup and take this bread and assimilate me unto yourselves."

Let our prayer be that we shall assimilate the Christ so completely this week that His vitality and His strength shall be ours —and above all, His Love and Joy and Humility and Trust shall be an actual part of us. Pray that we shall be worthy to be completely filled with Christ and because of that more capable to do His work.

Sincerely yours,

Glenn Clark

THE SIXTH BATH:
BATHING THE INNER TISSUES

In Lesson Three you were told how all life takes its rise in water. Read that lecture again.

According to Dr. William A. O'Brien, "An adult requires about three quarts of water per day, one quart to drink and two quarts supplied in food. Normally it is not necessary to keep a record of how much water is taken each day, as thirst is a reliable guide. All the chemical reactions of the body take place in watery solution. Body temperature is regulated by the amount of water which is evaporated from the skin surface. Water is of value in the healing of wounds. There is a great deal of water in our food, for most vegetables and fruits contain excessive amounts. Oranges, carrots, peaches, and tomatoes are made up of between 85 and 95 per cent water. Milk is 85 per cent water. Another source of water is the burning of foods in the body (oxidation). Drinking water with meals is not likely to do harm if it is not used to wash down partially chewed food. Under normal conditions, when water reaches the stomach it passes over the food mass, and does not mix with it. Drinking ice water or chilled water to relieve thirst is not necessary, as all water is adjusted to body temperature as it reaches the stomach. Part of the extra water finds its way out by way of the urine, but this does not cause any damage to the kidneys. If the body needs water for cooling purposes, much of the excess water appears as perspiration. In case of doubt concerning purity of water it should be boiled; the resultant flat taste can be eliminated by pouring the water through the air from one container to another."

Everyone is accustomed to drinking a glass of water after he has brushed his teeth, and before he goes to breakfast. If he suffers from constipation or headaches or if there is any other particular sluggishness of the digestive tract it would be well to drink a pint of warm water with half a lemon squeezed into it, a half hour before breakfast each day. If he went to a regular Spa that features healing waters, he would be given a regular system of drinking which he would be required to follow meticulously. That would probably be two glasses an hour before breakfast; two glasses at ten o'clock in the morning; two glasses at two o'clock in the afternoon; and two more at five o'clock. At bedtime he might drink, instead, a glass of orange juice or some other fruit juice.

In a former lesson we learned how the healing power of the baths of Jordan comes from the twin combination of water and sunshine. For the internal bath this is accomplished by pure water and vitamin-bearing food. It is easy to determine which foods contain the most sunshine. You won't have to pay much attention to learned names, such as proteins and carbohydrates, etc., if you will look for the *color* of your food. The sun itself is a master-painter, painting with tints of glory everything it touches with its life-giving rays. It paints the carrots yellow, and the beets red, and the citrus fruits orange, and the leafy foods green. Try to avoid the white sugars, white salts, white starches, white rice and white flour as much as possible. Most food is made up from 50 to 90 per cent of water; but the primary purpose of food is to carry *sunshine* into the body. For that reason, the synthetic foods, and all foods known as starch foods are not as responsive to spirit as the sun-kissed fruits and the plant leaf vegetables filled with what is known as chlorophyll.

Starches and sugars and proteins are fine for carrying the body up a long stairway of solid growth until one is about twenty-four, but unfortunately they then proceed to start the same body down a long slide toward death. These foods build a solid body rather than a responsive one, nice and squatty and excellent for sliding downhill.

But if you don't care for skidding downward after you reach middle life and prefer to keep your body as permanently responsive as an airplane, light and buoyant enough to rise upward in a long, unobstructed flight for a long and efficient life, turn to the sun-kissed and water-filled foods.

Most of us build solid, stupid bodies which tire easily and require long hours of sleep.

To avoid this, eat less starch food, more proteins, and most of all, the chlorophyll foods. In other words, eat less pastries and meats and more vegetables and fruits and nuts.

Rufus Moseley kept young at eighty on raw peanuts, raw cabbage and raisins. He said that a raw potato will cure stomach ulcers better than any medicine. Brown Landone at ninety-five wrote, "When I use foods which contain chlorophyll—a couple of glasses of green leaf juice, for instance,—and do not load my body down with starches, but eat plenty

of responsive protein foods—then my body responds
to Spirit. Spirit manifests through it, so that I need
but one meal a day and only two or three hours of
sleep."

Both Landone and Moseley worked long hours
each day without fatigue.

Stanley Jones gets his chlorophyll from the top of
green grass molded into Viet tablets, and finds he
can speak three to five hours a day without fatigue
and turn out a book a year besides.

As you grow older you might like to try Brown
Landone's prescription for keeping the inner channels cleared through a bath of water and sunshine in
a unique form which he recommended above all
others. This, he claimed, was not only cleansing but
purifying. "For this purpose, take one half cup of
spinach juice (you can buy such juice at a grocery
store) and add one half cup of sweet milk and one
full cup of distilled water. No other kind of water is
valuable for this purpose. If there is no commercial
company selling distilled water in your locality, buy
it at a drug store. Within a week you will find new
lightness and vibrancy of body."

The more our cells become water-like and sun-like,
the newer and younger we become. A Russian scien-
tist has discovered that life can be extended from
seventy years to one hundred and twenty if we can
restore the liquid, the fluid, the water in the interlinear tissue between the organs of the body. But
the finest elixir that has ever been discovered to
generate this interlinear liquid is a lifted consciousness, a turning and becoming as a little child.

Professor Baldwin Smith believes that we may be

able to shuffle off our old bodies as a snake sheds its skin when we learn how to renew the flesh beneath. It has been discovered that every eleven months each cell in the body is displaced by a new cell. "Every cell thinks," said Edison. That being so, let us "think" our cells into newness and freshness.

We know we must drink plenty of water to supply pure fluids to our bodies. But do we remember to open the unseen channels and crevices, to let liquid seep into the interlinear tissues between the organs? This can take place only when we have gained a mind at peace and a heart lifted toward God, open to His inflowing spirit.

Pure water can be an instrument for remarkable healing when it is accompanied by an ideal state of consciousness. Some springs are famous for healing because of a quality that defies all analysis. It is as though some ancient seer or prophet may have blessed them. But we ourselves can add to the healing power of any water we drink by blessing it, for water is flowing and pliant even in the invisible sense. Indeed, it is such a remarkable "conductor" that no one dares turn on an electric light while standing in a bath tub. But it conducts spiritual power in an even more electrifying way.

The mother of Ernest Hemingway had a serious head injury which created a blood clot on the brain. The doctors told her that in the whole history of medicine no one had been known to recover from such an injury as hers. She prayed to heaven, and a vision came to her in the image of her deceased husband who had been a physician while on earth, telling her to place a glass of water at her bedside when she retired and he would medicate it from heaven. He told her to drink this water in the morning, then leave another glassful to be medicated during the day and drink at night. She followed this routine faithfully and prayerfully for a week and the clot was completely dissolved and absorbed. The conductor of this spiritual power was a glass of pure water plus an "ocean" of pure faith.

One may smile at this. One may scoff. One may call it superstition. But the fact remains that in this case water was made a vehicle through which faith and the healing power of God could flow definitely and specifically into a given need. Her physician could not understand her cure, although he has her record.

Whenever you take a drink of water why not ask Jesus thus to bless it for you! Yes, pure water can be a wonderful conductor for the healing love of God to enter and bless you. Water is a perfect replica of the subconscious mind, on the physical plane. Faith that is powerful enough and simple enough can do almost anything with water. The ocean is swayed by the appearance and the disappearance of the moon. Rain obeys the call of the powerful and simple faith which controls the rhythmic ceremonies of the Hopi Indians.

When Jesus blessed the water at Cana he may not have actually turned it into wine. Knowing its conductivity to power of any kind, he may have injected into it the inspiring, stimulating power of the Holy Spirit in complete contrast to the unholy alcoholic spirits which the guests had been imbibing before, with the result that the host exclaimed in amazement, "Thou has kept the good wine until now."

And now, read and experience the following allegory adapted from "A Meditation" by the Provost of the Cathedral of the Holy Spirit, Cumbria, Scotland:

"Just as the water we drink penetrates into every part of our body, so when we drink of the Holy Spirit, this Spirit penetrates into every area of our being. This might be more effective if you recited it out loud:

"As the Holy Spirit enters into each chamber of my being He carries His peace—the peace that follows surrender—"The peace of God that passeth all understanding." As His peace fills my mind, all anxiety and doubt fade away. They cannot remain where His peace is. For in this peace I realize that He makes all things work together for good for those who love Him. While He fills me with His peace, He also fills me with His love, that love from which I cannot be separated by any power on earth or in hell. As His love fills me, all fear dies, for perfect love casteth out fear.

"As He fills me with His peace and love, He fills me also with His joy. In His presence is the fullness of joy, and His joy no man taketh from me. Nothing can separate me from His love, therefore nothing can rob me of His joy.

"As He fills me with His peace and love and joy, He also fills me with His power; the power of His spirit, by which He makes all things new, and renews the face of the world.

"He pours out His power and peace and love and joy until He fills my whole being.

"He enters the chamber of my will. I surrender it into His hands, and He sets it as truly as the needle of the compass is set to point north. He sets my will true, to point in line with the Father's will, so that the will of God can flow through mine undeflected to its accomplishment.

"He enters into the chamber of my memory and fills it with His light and love. He opens all the cupboards and sees all that is past, all that I remember, all that I have forgotten, and all that I never have known. He knows from whence I come, He knows every link of every chain of cause and effect that has gone into the making of me as I am.

"He enters into the chamber of my affections. I give them into His power. He disentangles my desires from all that is unworthy of a child of God, and sets my affections truly on things above, on all that is good and joyous and well-pleasing in God's sight.

"He enters the chamber of my understanding and fills me with that deep inner knowledge of God which is eternal life—knowledge too deep for intellect to grasp, the knowledge of growing intimacy.

"As He fills my mind, He fills the organ of my mind, (my brain and nervous system). Every nerve comes to rest in His peace, and while it rests it is refreshed in the multitude of peace. Every nerve is attuned to its true note, and all the nervous system becomes harmonized—responsive and resonant—to the peace of God which is filling my mind. As the nerves rest, they are refreshed, restored, and recharged with the nerve-energy. All the reservoirs of vitality are refilled while I rest in the peace of God.

"As my nerves rest, they carry the message of peace and order to all my body. Every organ rests, every fibre rests, every cell rests. And as my body rests, all its workings become tempered in true proportions. Each organ works in quietness and order and peace and regularity. Each contributes its share to the harmonious working of the whole. All the work of the body becomes peaceful, regular, and harmonious; and gradually vitality and strength are restored to my whole body."

EXERCISES FOR LESSON IX

READING EXERCISE: Read Rebecca Beard's *Everyman's Search*.

DIET EXERCISE: Try carrying out a carefully regulated drinking regime and sensible diet this week.

MEDITATION EXERCISE: Follow the meditation patterns of the Provost of Cumbria, Scotland given in this chapter.

THE SEVENTH BATH: BATHING THE SKIN

Dear friend:

And now some may be asking, "Why did you put all this practical advice on breathing and exercises and diet and bathing in the last lessons of this course? If we had been practicing them for twelve weeks instead of four or five, we might be improving faster."

I put them last because I wanted to put first things first. I said, as you may recall, in introducing the first bath—the washing of the soul—that if you got that done completely enough, with one hundred per cent faith, you would not need any of the other baths to get cured. But because everything in this world is made by God and because everything in your body is but an outer replica of the inner image and likeness of the Creator, I hoped you would give to all the subsequent lessons the same devoted attention that you gave to the first four. For, rightly understood, everything in your body is a spiritual thing—your lungs, your muscles, your skin; and everything outside of you is also spiritual—the air, the water, the food.

An old adage is "Cleanliness is next to Godliness," so the last of the seven baths deals with the washing of the skin. I shall try to show you how it not only can make you clean, but can make you more Godlike at the same time.

Sincerely yours,

Glenn Clark

THE SEVENTH BATH:
BATHING THE SKIN

In the old days no one thought of taking a bath oftener than once a week. The farmer who went to a New York hotel on a Wednesday and was given a "room with bath" said forlornly, "It's too bad it isn't Saturday night." Nowadays many take baths every day, some every three days and some every four days. One can take one's choice. Hot baths are good to relax the nerves, and cold baths to stimulate the system. If one's physical condition is not in top form a cold bath may be harmful. So it is wise to warm the skin first and then step under a cold shower for only an invigorating moment.

Gandhi and Starr Daily and other spiritual leaders find that very hot baths have a spiritual effect. That is probably because hot water symbolizes the reaction of the heat of the sun on water, which is a process producing a mysterious healing quality.

Every home of the future should be built to furnish a place for a sunbath. The ultra violet rays of the sun have been proven to carry miraculous healing forces through the skin, penetrating the organs. As the direct impact of the sun's rays can do as much harm as good, if continued too long, twenty minutes is the ideal period for exposure to the sun or a sun-ray lamp. But one should begin with an even shorter period of exposure and watch for any signs of skin burn.

There is great value in exposing the body to the open air. Benjamin Franklin and Brown Landone were both strong advocates of air baths. They stood for fifteen minutes each day in their bedrooms with their bodies exposed. Landone insisted that the air should be moving in a current. This would be a difficult effect to produce under ordinary circumstances, indoors. But both moisture and elements of sunshine are always in the air, even under shelter.

I was asking the Lord how I could prepare a lecture for this lesson that would lift such a common function as bathing one's skin into a high spiritual experience, and while I was praying, a letter came to me from England. It was from someone who had learned a new secret of the healing process. This is a part of the letter:

"Some years ago I discovered, through inspiration arising out of a need, an interesting fact. I found that if I placed one hand, or both, very lightly over any part of the body which was ailing, and at the same time, gave attention to the feeling which permeated the whole of the part, this procedure, when practiced for a few minutes at a time as often as possible, awoke within that part a condition of healing, which in a very little while, healed the place.

"I healed myself successively of (1) some very bad chilblains, (2) fingers crushed badly in the door of a car, (3) a boil in the ear, (4) very bad headaches, (5) very tiresome pains in my legs which I had had ever since I could remember, and (6) countless small pains and irritations which, perhaps, had they been left unattended, might have been forerunners of something much worse.

"It was not, however, until comparatively lately that it occurred to me to use this practice daily, not only over parts of the body which suffered some kind of discomfort, but over the whole body, to see if I could raise its tone.

Upon trying this practice of healing over the whole body, for a few minutes each day (the practice can be done in bed comfortably, night and morning), I made for myself, in a very short space of time, a good body to live in. The results were at once so good that I knew it would become my duty to pass this practice on to the rest of mankind.

"I found that I had been entertaining, within my mind, ever since I could remember, wrong pictures about the body. I had thought of it as a dense, solid thing, shut off from all its environment, different from it. *I found that it was far from being shut off from that space in which it lives and moves, being, in fact, completely open to it, as open to it as a room would be which had no walls, no floor, no ceiling. I found that this space, in which we live and move, freely enters within the body, invades it and permeates it intimately, the whole of the time.*

"*To feel this is to experience the sensations of physical lightness and balance, the feeling of the form being made whole every moment and essentially young, joyous, happy, renewed, refreshed. To feel this is also to experience space as something vital, subtle, fresh, joyous, creative, from which the body, and through the body the mind, receives life and inspiration, continuously, ceaselessly.*

"Our bodies are forms through which we contact this world of space, forms in which we have, as humans, come to live for a brief while. But our bodies are, at present, like wireless sets gone wrong. They give us information which is mostly not intelligible to us because, by not having learned to tune in to the spiritual universe, we have lost contact with it. Being out of contact with this information, we drag these bodies into situations which they are not made to face, causing contractions and divisions to arise in them which make them feel defective.

"Our bodies (and all forms in space) are completely and intimately *permeated* by the medium in which they live and move, call it ether, light, space, God, it does not make any difference to its nature. A healthy body would be naturally acquainted, by feeling, with the fact of this constant permeation and penetration, from which arises lightness, correct weight and form, balance, buoyancy, constant strength and inspiration. But because our bodies are not whole, having been sabotaged in rearing, the condition of attention in them is one which has entirely lost contact with the feeling of permeation and penetration. Nevertheless the permeability and penetration of the entire body ought to be felt constantly, for it is what constitutes wholeness. *The state of wholeness is a state of complete surrendering of the form to the penetrating life all about us in air and sunshine and the life-giving elements of God.*

"If you study each part of your body in turn, *regularly,* you will, after a while, be able to find and experience this sensation as you live and move, without the help of your hands, over your whole body. This will be the sensation of wholeness or complete relaxation in which there is spontaneous alertness and perfect interest for life and living.

"If our bodies were whole, we would feel that they are completely permeated and penetrated by that vital space in which we live and move, that they are buoyed up and carried lightly by it, informed and kept whole by it. But because they are not whole, having been, as I have said, sabotaged in rearing, we have lost contact with this feeling of constant and complete penetration and permeation. With the help of our hands and of our attention we must set out to regain this contact.

"This practice of healing, therefore, points to an adventure, that of finding what we really are. What is our potential? Ought we to express God-likeness? Can we not express, at any rate, that completeness and perfection which are everywhere to be seen in nature?"

This friend in England has stumbled upon a great Truth. How can we apply it? Yes, how can we express this wholeness? By the simple step of opening our minds, our hearts, our lungs, yes, our very pores, to let this wholeness that is all about us—this light and this life of God—enter us, penetrate us, permeate us, take complete possession of every nook and cranny of our being.

The simplest and the most direct way is by exposing our bodies to the vast space all about us, to the sunshine and to the air, knowing as we do so that this vast, invisible thing called space is filled completely and wholly with that great Invisible Being that we call God. In other words, when we unclothe ourselves morning and night, think of ourselves as being wholly and completely immersed in God. And when you bathe your skin, think of Jesus' statement that He is the Water of Life, and let His compassionate, loving touch bring healing through every pore of your body.

In the previous lesson, this water of life permeated your inner being, now it permeates your outer being, making you every whit whole. In the previous lesson when we referred to vitamin-bearing foods it may have recalled to your mind Jesus' statement that He is the Bread of Life. Whenever you partake of food henceforth you will be assimilating Christ unto yourself.

Two lessons ago in your spiritual exercises and spiritual relaxations, your blood vessels were receiving the blood transfusions from the saving blood of Christ. Three lessons ago while breathing air you were drinking in God of the Infinite Spaces, as in this lesson you are letting God of the Air bless your outer skin with healing.

God is always sound and well. God is never sick. He is all about you, above you, beneath you, within you. God is perfection. No one—try as he can—is able to escape God. Therefore, not one of us, if we can turn in love toward God and man, should be able to escape being healthy and well.

Now in conclusion listen very carefully: *There is no escaping perfection.* Jesus commanded us to be perfect even as our Father which is in Heaven is perfect. The only perfection is in the mind of God and the nearer we come to the mind of God and the more perfectly our will rests in His will without any exertion of our own—merely by surrender—the more completely perfection will be ours.

"Only one thing is needful," said Jesus to Martha. That is all. One thing! Union with God! And the rest can go, the strain, the heartbreak, the despair. Keep close to God and perfection will appear of itself, yes, in every cell of your body, as easily as a picture is brought to light when the photographic film is developed in the right chemicals.

The right chemicals for healing are the Seven Baths of Jordan. You have taken them all. You should be perfectly healed.

Hold that thought. Trust God completely. Trust the chemical action, the spiritual orchestration of sun and water, of Love and Trust, of Joy and Humility, the healing alchemy that produces perfection, that produces health. Trust the honesty and sincerity of your attempts to take these baths. Recognize the fact that you yourself have to do nothing. Think of yourself as the Temple of the Living God. Treat it with reverence. In that reverent mind immerse yourself in these baths, surrender yourself to them. In doing so surrender yourself to God, find unity in Him: then perfection will come to every cell in your body and every thought in your mind.

Trust, trust, trust.

EXERCISES FOR LESSON X

READING EXERCISE: Read Rebecca Beard's *Everyman's Mission*.

MEMORIZING EXERCISE: Review the memorized passages from former lessons.

MEDITATION EXERCISE: Morning and evening for a week try the exercise suggested by the friend from England.

If you have an ailment that needs special treatment here is the best therapeutic use you can make of water:

Father Knipe was the first man to use water in packs and baths to aid his parishioners in times of illness. He produced results that were remarkable to people of those days who were not used to thinking of water as a healing agent.

He considered the wet girdle as practically a panacea. The use of this pack by anyone trying to regain health is very beneficial. Use for pack, toweling—cotton toweling, not turkish. Have a long strip, double—sufficient to go around the body, lapping over the stomach area so that there are four thicknesses across the stomach. Follow this with a piece of rubber sheeting, the same length and width. Then a piece of wool blanket, same size. Wet the pack in cold water and wrap snugly about the body, then the sheeting and last the wool, pinning securely and tightly about the body. Apply this upon retiring, and wear it all night. Should you awaken and wish to remove it during the night, do so, then wash the body with fresh water, and go back to sleep. This can be used every night. It can also be applied at any time during the day and, since it is well wrung out, one can walk around and do a few things while helping the body: just be sure you are in a warm robe and keep warm. One should never allow the body to become cold during a pack. The body should be warm when the pack is applied. The area where the wet girdle is applied contains all of your organs with the exceptions of the heart and lungs—cool this area, and stimulate the organs to better functioning.

A like pack should be applied around the head for headache, around the throat in case of sore throat, etc. Do not stop using the pack as soon as the throat is better. The tissue has been scarred and needs help to become normal. You say you can take an aspirin for a headache, but when you realize that it takes the body eight days to throw off the poison produced by one aspirin, does this appear to be the wise way to handle the condition? All drugs produce toxic poisoning, as do all wrong emotions and wrong food combinations.

Lesson XI

THE MIGHTY LEVERS OF PRAYER

Dear friend:

When in all history has there been a greater amassing of knowledge of man and the universe than in these last fifty years? Through psychiatry nearly all the mysteries of the subconscious realm have been brought to light and yet what more have we learned about man's soul than our ancestors knew! For years we have been flying through the air, and now we are shooting pictures through the air. For years we were harnessing waterfalls to turn great turbines, and now we harness the split atoms to fight our battles for us. We are setting in motion powers such as our forefathers never dreamed of. But how few of us have learned that the power of prayer is greater than the radio and the power of love greater than the atomic bomb?

In this lesson I shall try to show you how we can bring the same efficiency into the psychological and spiritual realm that the world has achieved in the realm of matter. Fifty years ago Steinmetz, the great electrical wizard, the author of over three hundred wonderful inventions, made the statement, "For the past fifty years we have been working with the laws of matter. Fifty years from now we shall be making a study of the laws of spirit. When that time comes, we shall take Love into the laboratory and find more power in Love than there is in electricity. When prayer is used with the same confidence that we now use the forces of matter we shall achieve more in one generation than the world has achieved in the last four hundred years."

The fifty years are now up. In the Camps Farthest Out we have actually taken Love and Prayer into the laboratory and through them we have witnessed miracles as great as the miracles of the radio and the atomic bomb. The purpose of this lesson is to show you how to use some of these mighty levers of prayer.

Sincerely yours,

Glenn Clark

THE MIGHTY LEVERS OF PRAYER

In these last two lessons I am going to try to reveal the two greatest discoveries of my life. The first is Elisha's secret code of prayer. The second is Abraham's secret code of relinquishment. Five thousand years before I got the vision of a Camp Farthest Out Elisha got the vision and put it into operation under the title of the School of the Prophets. In the sixth chapter of the second book of Kings we catch a glimpse of how this movement, once started, began to grow and expand.

"This place is too small for us," said one of the young men. "Let us all go down to the river Jordan and each cut down a tree and build a larger camp."

This is so characteristic of any vital movement for developing the deeper phases of prayer life—to spread and expand. The very year that I am completing this book the Camp Farthest Out, which began in 1930 as a tiny camp at a Minnesota lake, has already expanded into forty-three camps covering the length and breadth of the nation and overflowing into Canada and Mexico. Next year we anticipate there will be fifty, including new ones springing up in Europe and Asia.

People gathered at the School of the Prophets as at the Camps Farthest Out to solve problems. The only problem described in the first seven verses of chapter six in Second Kings was the problem of finding a lost axe head which had flown from its handle while a young man was erecting the camp. The technique that Elisha used to bring that axe head to the surface of the water where it could easily be recovered reveals the secret code of prayer which Elisha used and which we have used with marvelous results in the Camps Farthest Out ever since they were founded. It consists of two steps.

The first step was revealed in Elisha's question, "Where did you lose it?" This is the same question that Jesus asked of the father of the epileptic boy. "When did this first begin?" It is the question which the skilled psychiatrist asks. "When did this complex first take root in your subconscious?"

When I came to St. Paul in 1912 a woman in the next block was dying of cancer of the throat. She had been to all the leading specialists and had been to Mayo Clinic and Johns Hopkins, and the verdict of all was the same: "In six months you'll be in your grave." As a last resort she went to an old lady who believed in prayer. One day the old lady said, "There must be someone you hate."

"There certainly is. I can't even think of her without feeling sick all over."

"Well, you will have to forgive her or there is no use in praying for you."

"I will never forgive her," and she flung out of the lady's presence and returned home. That night her husband asked her what the verdict was, and she told him. He said nothing but when they were ready for bed that night he said, "Let us kneel down beside the bed and have a prayer." He put his arm around her waist and said, "Now we are not going to get up from our knees until you have forgiven that woman."

"Then we'll kneel here all night," she replied. But before morning she gave up and forgave that woman, and forty years later when I was addressing a churchful of people in Coral Gables, Florida, whom did I see sitting on the front row but this same woman looking almost as young as she did forty years before. People now come to her when they need prayer.

One day a woman came to me who had not been able to hold the food that she ate longer than two or three minutes. She had been able to hold only four meals in the last four years, and the only way she survived was to try to eat ten meals a day. "Where did this begin?" I asked. She proceeded to confess all the little resentments and prides and selfishness and especially her disgust with certain people. Nausea is the stomach's reaction to food when one is disgusted about something. She was beginning to get close to the place where she had lost her power of assimilating what she ate. Suddenly the secret was brought to light, "When I married, I was afraid if I got too fat my husband would stop loving me."

"Ah, ha," I said. "Your subconscious heard you say that, and the subconscious of each person is the most loyal, devoted servant anyone could possibly desire. Like a dog faithful to its master it will obey any command without arguing or even understanding the reason why it is given. It will do anything to protect its master. I can almost hear your subconscious assert, 'I will see that she doesn't get too fat.' And it certainly has. It has done such a thorough job that you haven't got any fat on your bones at all!"

Then I turned to her and asked, "Are you afraid your husband would stop loving you now if you got too fat?"

"No!" she exclaimed. "He has been loving me through thick and thin, and I know nothing would change him now."

Hearing this I proceeded to carry on a silent conversation with her subconscious. "Now madam subconscious," I said in effect, "you must listen to me. First of all, I want to thank you for being such an obedient and watchful guardian over what you thought was the welfare of your mistress. You certainly did a wonderful job in preventing her from adding any flesh to her bones, but now she wants very much to add some flesh. I hereby command you to help her to do it quickly. Those are your orders. See that you obey them."

Then I turned to the little lady and said, "You and your husband come to my hotel tomorrow morning and eat a great big breakfast."

From that moment she was cured, not only physically but spiritually. She became a leader of the spiritual life work in her city in the years that followed.

The second technique which Elisha used in his School of the Prophets is a method which we have adopted as our key method in the Camps Farthest Out. This technique is revealed in the sixth verse of Chapter Six of Second Kings where Elisha picked up a stick and tossed it into the water where the axe head had been lost. Following this act the axe head immediately rose to the surface. The hidden code concealed in this process is as follows: When weighing a problem, take hold of something in your own

experience that you can take hold of with clear cut
faith, and lay that faith upon the need at hand.
Notice that Elisha didn't pick up a straw that the
wind would blow away nor did he grip an immense
Sequoia tree that would be too big for his hands, but
he seized a stick that fitted his hands perfectly. Jesus
used this method constantly in his use of parables.
He presented to each person who came in need a
situation that paralleled in his practical life the need
he had to meet, and when he applied the faith which
he had in the thing he knew, to the problem whose
solving he did not know, a miracle happened.

A woman, for instance, despairing of creating
harmony among three persons in her home was reminded that as a little leaven placed in three meas-
ures of meal would leaven a whole loaf, in the same
way real, sincere, unselfish love placed in these persons would eventually leaven the entire home.

There was a woman who had a constant flow of
blood that the surgeons at Johns Hopkins and Mayo
Clinic could not hem up. The reason was that she
could not reach either hospital. They were too far
away for her to reach—not in space but in time. As
a matter of fact they were two thousand years away.
There was one thing, however, that her faith could
take hold of and that was that torn clothing (and
she had made most of the clothes for her own family) could easily be hemmed up by anyone who loved
the garments enough to take the time to do the mend-
ing. If that was the case why could not bodies also
be hemmed up when the need called. She had never
seen a garment which she admired more than the
garment, all of one piece and woven from above,

worn by the Man of Galilee. Having heard him say that if a son asked for bread a human father would not give him a stone, therefore one could count positively on the fact that a far kinder heavenly Father would not decline any honest request from a child of His.

And so she built her "lever of faith" after this fashion: "If the woman who made Jesus' garment loved it enough to hem it so perfectly, why would not a loving Father love my body He made enough to hem it up when that is my pressing need?" Then she said to herself, "If I could only touch the hem of that garment with the same faith that Elisha seized the stick which fit his hand, I KNOW that my hemorrhage would cease. . . . But, alas, if I had the audacity to seize the garment of a man of God the crowd would denounce me as a woman of the street and stone me to death." She was about to give up the idea as hopeless when she saw the Man of Galilee start through a crowd packed so closely together that a daring idea came to her. "If I kneel behind that group of women yonder, where he will soon be passing, I may be able to reach beneath their gowns far enough to touch the hem of that garment and no one will know it." So she tried, and so she succeeded, and the rest is history. We shall always remember the words of Jesus, "Somebody touched me," and "Thy faith hath made thee whole."

In 1951 at the Camp Farthest Out in Texas a woman came to me and said, "I have a continuous inner hemorrhage. Will you pray for me?" "Come into the Prayer Room," I replied. And there before the painting of Christ, "The Presence," by Sallman,

I asked her to kneel while I told her the story of the woman of Galilee. Then I said, "I have seen Mr. Sallman paint his pictures. He puts love into each one, but his love can't hold a candle to the love which God puts into the making of human bodies. Note how carefully the garment in this picture is hemmed up by the painter's brush. Now with the same faith of the woman of two thousand years ago reach forward and touch the hem in that picture and Roberta Fletcher (the prayer hostess who has accompanied us) and I will pray for you." When we finished praying the woman was completely healed.

Two months later in the Minnesota Camp Farthest Out a woman said, "I must leave at once for California. Ever since my daughter's second baby came she has had a continuous inner hemorrhage. Today I received this letter, 'I just came from the doctor. He said my blood count is getting so low it won't be safe to wait any longer. I must be operated on next week.' "

I took the woman into the chapel where a picture of Sallman's "Christ Among The Sheep" was hanging. I told her of the woman of Galilee two thousand years away, and of the woman of Texas two thousand miles away, and asked her to stand on her tiptoes and touch the folds of the garment in the picture while I prayed for her daughter. When I had finished I suggested, "Instead of taking the plane, why don't you send an airmail letter asking for complete details, and an immediate reply? I believe you will find your daughter is healed." Four days later a letter came, saying, "I just came from the doctor's. He said, 'The hemorrhage evidently stopped two days ago.' All my organs are now perfectly sound. So I won't need an operation!"

The next year I was telling of this experience to an audience in the Oregon Camp Farthest Out and a woman arose and said, "I am the one you prayed with. I want to say that the hemorrhage never returned, and today I received a letter from my daughter stating that her third baby has just arrived, and everything was perfect and sound."

A woman came to me one day who had a tumor and a goiter, and her physical vitality was so low that the doctors said an operation would be fatal. As Jesus clothed his "levers" in parables, I tried to speak to her need by means of a parable.

"The Kingdom of Heaven is likened to a Mrs. Smith who had a little Ford car and a little Ford garage and was perfectly happy until Mrs. Jones next door bought a big Cadillac car and put it into her big Cadillac garage. Now Mrs. Smith didn't need a Cadillac, but she wanted to keep up with the Joneses so she began to want one, and she wanted it so hard that after a while she got one. She tried to put it into her garage but it was too long so it stuck out. Where it sticks out, we will call that a growth. Can you think of anything in your past life that you passionately wanted, but that was not in your divine plan to have?"

"Yes," she replied, "and when I couldn't have it, it made me feel sick all over. Ever since then I have been trying to forget it."

"If it is something that didn't belong in your life, you should completely relinquish it and not tuck it away deep in your subconscious and merely try to forget it. A man who is timid about having his infected tooth pulled and tries to forget it will find it manifesting later on as rheumatism. Your trying to forget this frustration is the worst thing you could do. It is now manifesting in these growths. Are you willing to tell me what it was you so earnestly desired and could not have?"

When she told me, I said, "Are you now willing to relinquish it?" When she said she was, I threw open the window and said, "Let us toss it out into the hands of God right away." Then turning to her I handed her a little booklet of mine called, *The Lord's Prayer.* "In this booklet," I said, "there is a chapter entitled 'The Divine Plan.' Take this book and read that Divine Plan regularly every morning for the next three weeks and I will pray for you with power." When the three weeks were up she wrote me, "The doctor has just taken an X-ray. He said my goiter and tumor are vanishing away, and I won't need an operation."

That was the incident that lead me to write *How To Find Health Through Prayer,** in which I listed the emotional causes behind most of the diseases. Several years after that book was published, magazines all over the nation began announcing the new discovery of the medical profession, called psychosomatics, in which the emotional causes behind diseases were listed almost exactly the way I had listed them.

* *How To Find Health Through Prayer,* Glenn Clark, Harper, New York. $1.75

A woman came to me in great need. She said she had a hundred gallstones in one side and a growth in the other and terrible headaches.

Following Jesus' custom, as was my wont, I tried using a parable. Knowing that this woman was very familiar with the uses and capacities of the vacuum cleaner, I called her attention to the fact that years ago they used to have vacuum cleaner wagons, and for the payment of $25.00 the wagon would come to one's home and a half dozen men with long hoses would in a few hours clean the house from top to bottom, thus saving the housewife three weeks of hard work.

Then I said, "Let us invite the Lord to send his celestial vacuum cleaner wagon down here and let His healing angels enter in and draw from your body all the poisons, toxins, and infections that may be hidden there. As these angels are invisible, let them penetrate into the most hidden pockets and nooks and crannies until all the poisons are drawn out. At the same time let us ask Him to send another set of healing angels into your subconscious mind to draw out all the frustrations, fears, and resentments that may be lodging there. As these angels neither slumber nor sleep let them keep on the job all night, all the next day and, if necessary, all week, yes, all month until the job is done. Let them go down the corridors of time clear to your babyhood and open hidden doors behind which may be concealed that fright of your babyhood and those frustrations of youth and resentments of middle age, those hidden frustrations and resentments that you may have forgotten." Then I added, "But, dear Father, don't let them work too fast as we don't want them to cause any pain. And now let your healing love flow in, and touch up all the sore places and fill all the vacant places. Thank you, Father, in Jesus' name, Amen."

When I finished this informal prayer, she said, "I do not feel any different." But before the week was up she phoned me long-distance from Texas saying, "I just came from the doctor. He took an X-ray and wouldn't believe it so he took three more. All the gallstones are gone, the growth has entirely disappeared, and my headaches are a whole lot better."

Since then whenever I have led a prayer group, before I close I usually ask "How many present would like to be sent to the cleaners today?" The response is usually unanimous. Wonderful results have come from this little process of housecleaning so now that you have reached the close of this lesson, you will find the first exercise will be the applying of this vacuum cleaner to your own needs.

EXERCISES FOR LESSON XI

READING EXERCISE: I have already assigned all the books on healing I have in mind. But if you are giving three months to a course under my direction you probably have seen my autobiography, *A Man's Reach*.* In that case I suggest you read chapters twenty-two and twenty-three which relate my experience with the "Levers of Prayer."

MEMORIZING EXERCISE: Review passages already memorized.

MEDITATION EXERCISE: Let the Celestial Vac-

* *A Man's Reach,* Glenn Clark, Harper, New York. $3.00

uum Cleaner angels get busy drawing out all the
toxins, poisons, and infections from your body and
all the frustrations, fears, and resentments from
your subconscious mind. This is not wishful thinking, it is not play-acting, it is not mere superstition.
It is placing the most precious function of the entire
intellect, the inspired *imagination* completely into
the hands of God just as Jesus used to do when He
used parables to heal the people of Galilee. Remember the words of Jesus "Blessed are ye if ye hear
these words of mine and do them."

PRAYER EXERCISE: Try to find the right levers
for bringing cure to some ailment of your own or
the ailments of some friend.

THE SECRET
OF OVERCOMING DEATH

Dear friend:

People who are so full of Love, Joy, Peace, and Trust that there is no room in them for negative emotions to enter are the people who always keep well. They are also the people who can become splendid instruments for the healing of others.

The chief essential for spiritual healing is the capacity to love everything and fear nothing. We can overcome that which we do not fear, and we can command that which we love.

Jesus taught his followers how to overcome their enemies by the simple act of loving them, "Do good to them that hate you, and pray for them which despitefully use you, and persecute you" (Matt. 5:44). In Lesson III I showed how Jesus could command the demons to depart because he treated them kindly. Alcoholics can be healed by prayers not to stifle their craving but to welcome it as it is--a desire to lose themselves in a power greater than themselves and asking God to fill them with the Holy Spirit so completely that they will no longer be satisfied with spurious, counterfeit, make-believe, the unholy alcoholic spirits.

Jesus overcame death by having no fear of it. He referred to death as a friend when he said, "He who would save his life shall lose it." Great "healers" have no fear of death. A lion tamer who enters the ring with fear in his heart is in great danger of the powerful beasts around him, whereas he who goes as Helen Keller did into a lion's cage with no fear in her heart, is perfectly safe.

For that reason the greatest step you can take to insuring wholeness in yourself and bringing wholeness to others is to wipe out completely any lingering fear of death. The purpose of this lesson is to help you to do just that thing. When you can do that and put all your trust, unafraid, in God, then God can use you mightily for bringing healing to others.

Sincerely yours,

Glenn Clark

THE SECRET
OF OVERCOMING DEATH

In this last lesson I want to call your attention to the strangest paradox of all the paradoxes that Jesus gave us, and the one which, when properly applied, has the most potency of all when it comes to healing. "He that would lose his life shall save it."

How can it be that to be willing to die actually helps one to live? Note the words "to be willing to die," not *the desire to die.* The desire to live, if it be a genuine desire, planted deep within the subconscious, if, in the words of the psalmist, "all that is within you" is behind the desire, greatly increases your chances to live . . . provided . . .

Provided what?

Provided you have no fear of death. "What I fear," wailed Job, "has come upon me." Fear, like desire, is a magnet and draws unto itself that which it fears. If a man longs for death a small infection can take him quickly. If he longs for life and has no fear, a serious infection can be quickly overcome. But if his longing for life is equaled by his fear of death, the infection may cling to him for a long time.

It is easier to banish fear for oneself than for a loved one. That is the reason physicians never attend to their own families. "Professional courtesy" requires other physicians to do the job without charging a cent, so why not let the other fellow do the "dirty work?" But the reason goes far deeper than that. An outsider can treat one seriously ill with less personal fear than can a member of the family.

149

The purpose of this last lesson is to rid you, if possible, of all fear of death. It was not until I lost all fear of death that I became proficient in the healing of others.

Let me tell you how it was brought to me in the most convincing way that death is not a terrible thing but can become a great blessing for those who are left behind. When the *Soul's Sincere Desire* came out I noticed that Ellery Sedgwick, the editor of *The Atlantic,* had placed the following statement on the jacket of the book. "This is the personal record of a man who has learned to pray as naturally as to breathe and whose every prayer is answered." I said to my wife, who was very much opposed to publicity of any kind and especially exaggeration, "I am going to write Ellery Sedgwick to take that out," and was startled at her immediate reply, "No, Glenn, I wouldn't bother, for I have noticed that ever since your mother died three years ago all your prayers have been answered."

Then I recalled how my mother had great wishes for me but as long as she lived the tensions in her body and the inhibitions in her mind held these wishes in check, but the moment she stepped into heaven, the inhibitions and checks were removed and all her wishes were multiplied in power by infinity, and the things she wished for her children were now coming true.

Years later I met Starr Daily, and he told me how for twenty-five years he had lived in the underworld with nothing but hate in his heart and was pronounced by judges and psychiatrists as incorrigible. His father had spent a fortune trying to change him, protect him, and save him, but all to no avail. His father's great love for him was more on the horizontal plane than the vertical plane, more human and personal than celestial. When all his efforts had failed, and he saw Starr returned to the penitentiary for the last time as completely unrepentant and incorrigible as ever, the old father went home and in a short time stepped through the gates of heaven. Immediately afterwards all his wishes for his son's welfare, which had been so futile while he remained upon this earth, were multiplied in power by infinity, and the skies opened and the vision of Jesus Christ appeared before Starr as he lay exhausted in his solitary confinement cell. Never had Starr seen such love as he saw in the eyes of Jesus and that love literally drew all the hate out of him as completely as poison is drawn out of a wound. From that moment Starr was a redeemed man.

When Stephen was being stoned he looked into the eyes of Saul of Tarsus, the efficient persecutor of the Christians and the greatest scholar of his time. Stephen had undoubtedly done a lot of "wishful thinking" to the end that some event would bring to a close Saul's terrible practice of breathing out "threatenings and slaughter against the disciples of the Lord," but as long as Stephen was on this earth all his prayers and wishes were futile. When he was being stoned he looked at the man standing by his clothes, the man whose persecution had brought him to his death, and with love and forgiveness in his heart he prayed "Lord, hold this not against them." And undoubtedly he whispered in his heart, "And some day bring this man to Thee." As soon as he stepped into heaven, his wishes, futile on earth, were multiplied in power by infinity and the voice of Jesus came to Saul just as the vision came to Starr Daily, and the complete change came to him that made him the Foundation Builder of Christendom.

During the thirty years that I was a teacher at Macalester College several hundred of the students got the impact of my message in ways that changed their lives. One day I made a careful survey of the three hundred who had caught this dynamic, quickening most powerfully and I was startled to find that everyone had an empty chair in his or her home. In every case but one it was a father or a mother or a brother or a sister who had gone to heaven and whose wishes for those left behind were being multiplied in power by infinity, and heaven's power was coming through that was not so available to those who had not had this experience. The one exception I referred to was a young man who had been given up to die by the doctors, and through our prayers had been brought back to wholeness and health. Does that mean that there are ways of opening the gates of heaven for the power and blessing to come through without having to have one's loved ones go completely out?

We do not have to depend upon our loved ones who have gone on before to help us, if we can take Jesus into our heart of love as profoundly as we love our own family, and go to Him directly for help. We should take literally that profound statement of his, "Greater works than I have done ye shall do because I go unto the Father." In that hour he explained to his disciples that he could really help them more from heaven than when on earth in a bodily form. He was implying in a more effective way than I have done that the moment he stepped into heaven all his wishes for those who believed in him would be multiplied in power by infinity and that he would be instantly available to help them whenever they needed him, not in the form of an individualized human body but in the form of the Holy Spirit.

The moment all fear of death left me a great power of overcoming death became mine. I discovered this when I cured myself of palpitation of the heart. I verified it when a woman told me that her son had infantile paralysis and six doctors had left the home saying he would not live through the day. I said to her, "If the President of the United States asked your son to be Secretary of State and sit at his right hand in the cabinet, you would not insist on keeping your boy at home would you?"

"No," she replied, "I would want whatever was best for the boy." Then I said, "If God asks him to come to heaven and sit at His right hand you must admit that heaven is a far better place than Washington."

An hour later she phoned me saying that she had spent the hour on her knees giving her son completely back to the Father. "I told Him," she said, "that he is not a son of mine; he is a son of God's, he is just loaned to me. I am willing to accept with radiant acquiescence whatever is best for the boy."

In three months the boy was back in school without even a limp.

Within a year following this hearing eighteen cases were brought to me of children who had been given up for death and in every case where the parents completely relinquished the child to the Father without fear of death they recovered. Two of these were my own daughters who had been afflicted with scarlet fever and after three weeks the crises turned to the worst. Their throats closed to such an extent they could not drink water, and just one degree farther they would not be able to breathe. Ambulances were brought to the house and the two little girls were rushed to the contagious ward of the hospital where the parents could not follow them. My wife put her arms around me and said, "Glenn, you have told these other parents they must give their children back to the Father and now we must be willing to do the same thing. I myself had scarlet fever and rheumatic fever and it has left me with a weak heart so I have to go through life like a bird with a broken wing. I am not sure that I want my lively little girls to go through all the restrictions and limitations that I have had to go through. Rather than have them go through life crippled I would be willing that God take them to heaven if that is His plan."

"Let us give them completely into the kingdom," I replied, "if that is what would be best for them; but let us put our prayer in this form: Lord, we are willing to give these children into the Kingdom of Heaven if You desire them, but my wife and I are giving a pledge right now that we are going to try to make our home so nearly like the Kingdom of Heaven that if it won't make any difference to You, we would be very happy to have You let them find that Kingdom right here and now. In the name of the loving Son, Amen."

Three weeks later when those little girls returned from the hospital they had the glow of heaven in their eyes, and I am not sure but that this experience of looking into the gates of death, and being relinquished into the Loving Power of God so completely, is one of the reasons why they have grown into such angelic wives and madonna-like mothers.

But what if the patient dies after she has been completely relinquished into the Lord's hands? Then a great—perhaps a greater—blessing is hers. That is the way the great martyrs died. All the records of history show how the power of a cause is not weakened but strengthened by the death of its leaders. "The blood of the martyrs is the seed of the church," are not idle words. The crucifixion of Jesus was not the end of Christianity but its beginning.

The purpose of this lesson is not only to remove from you the fear of death, but to disclose the secret of multiplying the power of your prayers by infinity while you are yet living. Paul was the first one after Christ to discover that secret. Here it is in a nutshell: "I am crucified in Christ. I live and yet not I but the Christ in me." To be utterly surrendered to Christ, to be completely swept up in him, "hid with Christ in God," is to experience the secret. The prayers of Brother Lawrence, of St. Francis, of George Müller, of George Washington Carver were effective because "the little i with a dot over it had been crossed out on the outstretched arms of love."

The best substitute for dying is to lose oneself in Jesus. The next best substitute for dying is to lose oneself in the needs of others.

I was afflicted with a severe case of astigmatism from the time I was fourteen years of age. When I was forty-four I prayed that I would be healed so I could be liberated from wearing spectacles. After these prayers brought no change I ceased praying for my own physical needs and prayed only for others. Ten years later, at the age of fifty-four I found my astigmatism was gone.

When Mrs. Alexis Carrel was a nurse at Lourdes she lifted a woman, who was in the throes of death, so she could breathe better. The woman looked across the room and saw a patient in such pain that she forgot herself and started praying for this other patient. As she did so, the cancerous tissue sloughed off and she was instantly healed.

The more completely one can let go of one's need after placing it in the hands of God, the more completely God can take care of it. The ones who have most completely surrendered their wills to God, and have most completely lost themselves in others are the ones who can let go their problems most completely into the hands of the Father.

Many are the devices I have resorted to for helping folks "let go." One is to open the Bible and say, "Lay your problems on the promises of God, but don't lay them there if you are going to take them up again." Amazing answers have come when people have laid their problems in perfect trust upon the precious promises in that Book, and gone off and left them. When you take a pair of shoes to the shoemaker to be half-soled you go off and leave them, don't you? How otherwise would the shoemaker be able to mend them? Likewise, how can God get at our problems if we continue to hug them to ourselves? Yes, the biggest problem in prayer is how to "let go and let God."

A friend of mine, George V. McCausland, when faced with a particularly difficult problem, writes it down and closes it between the pages of his immense old family Bible, and leaves it there. That gave me a brilliant idea. Listen to it carefully, for I believe if you follow the directions faithfully you will get some wonderful results.

When I was a boy raising chickens I had one old hen whom I called "Mrs. Speckle," whose batting average when it came to hatching eggs was better than Babe Ruth's in knocking home runs. I would place thirteen eggs under her, and twenty-one days later, twelve would be transformed into lively, happy little chirping chickens. I didn't have to do anything about it. I turned the entire job over to Mrs. Speckle. Here is where my brilliant idea came in: Why can't we put as much trust in God as I put in an old hen?

Now to elaborate the idea. Take a sheet of paper and draw thirteen eggs and write upon each one the name of some person you want to pray for, or some problem you want to pray about. Then open your old family Bible to chapter ninety-one of the Psalms and lay the entire setting of "prayer eggs" between its pages. Then place the Bible back upon the shelf and leave it there for twenty-one days. Mark the date on the calendar to which you can look forward expectantly and joyously for the hatching of your brood.

Don't strain your ears to listen for a peep until the twenty-one days are completely up. Put as much trust in God and His assuring promises as you do in the old hen and her sheltering wings.

When the twenty-one days are up at last, then, and not till then, start counting the answers to your prayers. You may find one or two are not answered. The reason for these failures may be traced back to the same two causes that prevented eggs from being hatched. One is that the egg was rotten in the first place. When a prayer has a taint of ego, vanity, jealousy, greed, or escape from reality, it is not a sound prayer. The other reason eggs don't hatch is that they slip out from under the wings and become exposed to the cold air outside. When a person keeps pulling his prayers out from the Secret Place of the Most High and worries about them, he is preventing the warm love of a Heavenly Father from getting in its full work.

Finally, when the downy little creatures do appear, don't be disappointed if they don't crow and cackle and lay eggs the very first day. Give them time to grow and mature and feel their wings. When a prayer is answered, it often requires years of growth before it is experienced in all its power and beauty.

When the three weeks are up, place the list in the thirteenth chapter of Luke for a month or more and let Jesus brood over the little fledglings in His loving way.

The reason why I suggested Luke thirteen is that it was there that Jesus resorted to the same analogy that I have resorted to, that of the broody hen: "Oh

Jerusalem, Jerusalem, which killest the prophets, and stonest them that are sent unto thee; how often would I have gathered thy children together, as a hen doth gather her brood under her wings, and ye would not!" Luke 13:34.

The reason why I suggested Psalm ninety-one was that there the psalmist used the analogy of the mother eagle hatching and caring for her young: "He shall cover thee with his feathers, and under his wings shalt thou trust: his truth shall be thy shield and buckler." Psalm 91:4.

Dwell upon some of the precious promises in this greatest of all the Psalms in the Old Testament:

"Because thou hast made the Lord, which is my refuge, even the most High, thy habitation, there shall no evil befall thee, neither shall any plague come nigh thy dwelling." Psalm 91:9, 10.

"He shall call upon me, and I will answer him: I will be with him in trouble; I will deliver him, and honour him. With long life will I satisfy him, and shew him my salvation." Psalm 91:15, 16.

Yes, He will hear and answer you.

In my childhood chicken business, I made it a point not to disturb Mrs. Speckle during those twenty-one days. I knew that, by some strange instinct known only to God, she was far more capable of doing the job than I was. Now that I have become a man, I have discovered that I can trust God and the precious promises in the Bible to do this job far better than I can.

We don't need more people in the chicken business, but we do need more people in the prayer business.

The four points I wish you would carry away permanently from the reading of this lesson are:

First: Lose all fear of death by realizing that Heaven is infinitely more glorious than earth and the power released there is far greater than anything mere humans can experience.

Second: Die to the little self through utter surrender to the heavenly Father, so that His unlimited power can flow through you as through a channel.

Third: Lose yourself in serving others. This not only blesses others but heals the blesser. The moment one ceases to think of self he is whole. Even a cripple or a blind person, for whom there is no possibility of cure, ceases to be aware of his infirmity, indeed he almost rejoices in it, the moment he ceases to think of self in his joy in thinking of others. From that moment a unique type of wholeness is his.

Fourth: Follow this losing of self in Christ and in others by "letting go" completely and utterly of every request and wish and prayer into the hands of the Father.

EXERCISES FOR LESSON XII

READING EXERCISE: Read *God's Reach*.

MEMORIZING EXERCISE: Review the memorized passages of past weeks.

PRAYER EXERCISE: Pray over and over again one little phrase in the Lord's Prayer: "Thy Kingdom come and thy will be done on earth *as it is in heaven.*" For this week concentrate on prayers for others and try forgetting yourself—"hid with Christ in God."

Place a setting of eggs in the ninety-first Psalm following directions literally as given in this lesson.

AFTERWORD

Now that the seven baths are finished, my parting advice to you is that you start at the beginning and take it all over again. But instead of reading it straight through as a book, as you have probably done this first time, I suggest you read only one chapter a week and follow it with the assigned reading of the other books before you take the new chapter. And as you read, give your chief attention to putting the basic principles into practical action. Remember how a greater Teacher than I said once, "Whosoever heareth these sayings of mine, and doeth them, I will liken him unto a wise man, which built his house upon a rock: And the rain descended, and the floods came, and the winds blew, and beat upon that house; and it fell not: for it was founded upon a rock."

This has been a lovely little fellowship together. Our prayers have intermingled as well as our thoughts. Now my prayer is for wholeness to be yours in God's perfect way.

GLENN CLARK

BE THOU MADE WHOLE

BOOKS BY GLENN CLARK

Come, Follow Me

God's Reach

A Man's Reach

Fishers of Men

What Would Jesus Do?

I Will Lift Up Mine Eyes

The Soul's Sincere Desire

Two or Three Gathered Together

The Way, the Truth, and the Life

How to Find Health Through Prayer

BE THOU MADE
WHOLE

BY

Gᴌᴇɴɴ Cʟᴀʀᴋ

ST. LUKE'S PRESS
2243 FRONT ST.
SAN DIEGO 1, CALIF.

MACALESTER PARK PUBLISHING COMPANY

SAINT PAUL   MINNESOTA

CPSIA information can be obtained at www.ICGtesting.com
Printed in the USA
LVOW102130060912

297643LV00003B/400/P

9 781162 919492